Path to Bliss
A Practical Guide to Stages of Meditation

Path to Bliss
A Practical Guide to Stages of Meditation

H. H. the Dalai Lama, Tenzin Gyatso

Translated by Geshe Thubten Jinpa
Edited by Christine Cox

Snow Lion Publications
Ithaca, New York

Snow Lion Publications
P.O. Box 6483
Ithaca, New York 14851
U.S.A.

Printed in USA

ISBN 0-937938-92-0

Library of Congress Cataloging-in-Publication Data

Bstan-'dzin-rgya-mtsho, Dalai Lama XIV, 1935–
    Path to bliss : a practical guide to stages of meditation / H.H.
the Dalai Lama, Tenzin Gyatso ; translated by Geshe Thubten Jinpa ;
edited by Geshe Thubten Jinpa and Christine Cox.
    p.   cm.
Translated from Tibetan.
Translation based on oral discourses.
Includes bibliographical references and index.
ISBN 0-937938-92-0
    1. Lam-rim.   2. Blo-bzaṅ-chos-kyi-rgyal-mtshan, Panchen Lama I,
1567?–1662.   I. Thubten Jinpa.   II. Cox, Christine.   III. Title.
BQ7645.L35B78   1991
294.3'443–dc20   90–26250
                                                           CIP

Contents

Preface

The system of meditation known as Lamrim, stages of the path
to enlightenment, was begun by the great eleventh-century
saint-scholar Atisha and has been developed over successive
generations by Tibetan meditators. It originated with Atisha's
eloquent work in verse appropriately titled *Lamp for the Path
to Enlightenment*, in which he condensed the essence of the
entire Buddhist training of the mind in the stages of mental
development suitable to the trainees of initial, middling, and
highest capacity. The great scholar and adept Tsongkhapa
based his much admired text *Lamrim Chenmo* (Great Exposition on the Stages of the Path to Enlightenment) on this clas-
sic work; it explores in great depth the subject matter of
Atisha's *Lamp*.

As was the original intent of the authors, the beauty of Lamrim lies in its systematic approach to training the mind through
meditative contemplation, taking into account the complex-
ity of the human mind. With Lamrim practice, one embarks
upon a fresh spiritual journey in uncovering the layers of mists
that obscure the human personality. Its approach is simple,
rational and yet profound and does not presuppose any knowledge or training on the part of the beginner. The example of

many great meditators testifies to the efficacy of the Lamrim system. Beginning with elementary trainings, such as how to adopt a sound and right mental outlook and motivation in one's life, it leads the practitioner to the profound discovery of the reality, emptiness, that underlies the entire expanse of phenomena. Such an insight brings into question the very basis and validity of many of our strongly held conventional beliefs which are at the root of all our fluctuating emotions, thus showing the discrepancy between the way things are and how we perceive them to be. This revelation, when developed with the bodhisattva motive of universal compassion to work for the benefit of all beings, comes into its perfection in a state beyond duality and conceptuality. It is the state of full enlightenment, where the individual is free of all limitations and has brought his or her human potential to its fullest development, so as to be of limitless service to his or her fellow beings.

Path to Bliss: A Practical Guide to Stages of Meditation is a translation, based on an oral teaching of H.H. the XIVth Dalai Lama, of Panchen Lobsang Choekyi Gyaltsen's Lamrim, titled *Path to Bliss Leading to Omniscience*. The teaching was given at the main temple in Dharamsala, India, in the spring of 1988 together with several other discourses. The translation was first done simultaneously at the teaching, and was then later corrected by comparing it to the Tibetan tapes. As the type of commentary given on the text at the discourse was experiential in nature, the tradition requires four repetitions of the main sections of the practices. These repetitions have been incorporated in this book into a single body, thus presenting the entire teaching in an easily readable, yet complete, written form.

A brief note is owed to the reader on the editing of His Holiness' original teaching. Being a commentary on the First Panchen Lama's Lamrim, the original format of His Holiness' teaching followed the structure of that text in which all the main Lamrim meditations were explained within the framework of the preliminary, main, and concluding practices. However, in this book the format has been altered a little to suit the needs of both readers and practitioners. The book is divided into three parts. Part I is comprised of a general introduction to the spiritual path of a Buddhist practitioner and the origins of the Lamrim instructions. Part II deals with the elements of preliminary practices within the framework of the six stages of preparation. It ends with an instruction on activities during the between-session periods and a summary note explaining how to integrate the preliminaries with the main Lamrim meditations. In Part III, all the main Lamrim meditations are explained by topic so that they can be either studied and practiced in conjunction with the preliminary practices found in the preceding chapters, or reflected upon independently. Since the practice of a bodhisattva's way of life is a crucial element in the Lamrim path, the procedure of the ceremony through which a bodhisattva trainee commits himself/herself to follow such an ideal is included in Part III. Other vital materials on the practices of a bodhisattva, such as the bodhisattva vows and precepts of thought transformation practice, are given in appendices. For readers who wish to cross-refer the sections of this book with the original Tibetan version of *Path to Bliss*, the translation of the outline of the original text is provided in Appendix III. In conforming to the spirit of His Holiness the Dalai Lama's personal approach to teaching, a certain style of language has been adopted in this book. Every attempt has been made to keep the language as clear and succinct as possible to convey the spirit of His Holiness' thoughts without compromising the accuracy of the translation. Notes and a glossary have been prepared to assist readers with the technical terms used in this book, and a brief bibliography has been provided for the texts cited in this work.

We would like to express our deep thanks to Mrs. Joyce Murdoch, who undertook the difficult task of making the initial transcript of the translation from the tapes. Our grateful acknowledgment is also due to Glenn Mullin, who permitted us to quote several verses from his translation of the Lamrim

preliminary rite in *Essence of Refined Gold* (Snow Lion, 1983).
It is our sincere wish that our humble service in bringing out
this book may be of benefit to many and that the noble aspirations of H.H. the Dalai Lama be fulfilled.

Thupten Jinpa
Christine Cox

**PART I:
INTRODUCTION**

1 General Introduction

All living creatures possess an innate notion of self based upon the aggregates of body and mind, a self that naturally desires happiness and wishes to avoid suffering. This natural instinct knows no boundaries, and pervades all forms of life in this universe, regardless of the external differences in the physical appearances of these forms. It is this urge that makes all of us hold ourselves most dear and precious. Because this instinct is a just one, the individual has a natural right to work for the achievement of happiness and the overcoming of suffering.

As mentioned in *Uttaratantra* (Unsurpassed Continuum), all beings further possess the potential to free themselves from the binding chains of suffering and anxiety. The presence of this potential strongly indicates the presence of the Buddha nature or the seed of full enlightenment inherent within all beings.

The factor that distinguishes humans from other living species is the ability to utilize intelligence while retaining the human qualities of love, kindness, and honesty towards fellow beings. It is vital for people with an appreciation of a deeper dimension of human nature not to let themselves be enslaved by materialism. It is possible to work for one's livelihood and yet not to stray from sincerity and honesty. Ironically, although the underlying aim of material development is the attainment of more happiness and peace, if one were to lead one's life totally occupied with material development alone and were to disregard the needs of one's spiritual life, the fulfillment of this basic aim probably would not be realized.

It is very obvious to us that the experiences of the mind are far more acute and strong than those of the body. Therefore, if the continuity of the mind remains even after death, then it becomes most essential for us to ponder upon our after-death fate. It is important to probe whether or not it is possible, on the basis of this consciousness, for an individual to achieve a permanent state of peace and happiness. If it is, then it becomes a matter of great personal concern for us to take the initiative to make the necessary efforts to arrive at such a state.

When we talk of conciousness superficially, it appears as though we were talking about a single entity. But if we analyze deeper we find that there are various types and levels of conciousness. Certain types of conciousness are undesirable in that when they arise they torment the individual's mind, but there are others whose arisal ushers in calmness and peace. So our task now is to discriminate skillfully between these two categories of consciousness. Generally speaking, consciousness is in the nature of clarity and knowing; it is susceptible to change and transformation. Therefore, the essential nature of consciousness is pure and clear, which suggests that the delusions that pollute the mind have not penetrated into its nature. All the mental stains, such as ignorance and the other delusions that often torment us, are adventitious and hence not indivisible aspects of our minds. Because these delusions, dualistic conceptions and so forth are unstable and reside only temporarily within our consciousness, they can be alleviated and eventually rooted out when their actual opponent forces are applied properly. The achievement of such a feat marks the attainment of a permanent peace and happiness.

As I often remark, in this world there are many different categories of people: those who adhere to some form of spiritual belief, those who are totally against it, and those who are just indifferent to religion. When people confront situations that defy rational explanation and that are adverse, they differ in their ability to cope with them. As long as those who do not believe in any spiritual system encounter situations that are within the scope of human understanding, they can cope with them. But any circumstances beyond their own understanding come as a shock, and their attempts to deal with them result in frustration and anxiety. A practitioner of *dharma* has a better understanding of life and therefore will not lose courage and hope, factors that are most vital for sustaining the force of life. Therefore, the importance of spiritual development in one's life is obvious; and in this respect, I believe that the Buddhist doctrine has much to offer.

There are many different ways of undertaking the practice of dharma; these vary from individual to individual. Some people can totally renounce the worldly way of life and choose the way of a hermit, devoting their entire time and energy to meditation. Others undertake their practice while maintaining a conventional life in the world. One should not have the wrong notion that the practice of dharma is to be put off for the future when one can set aside a specific time for it; rather, it should be integrated into one's life right now. The essence is to live one's life within the noble principles of the dharma and give a direction and purpose to one's life. If one can adopt such an outlook, the dharma will not only be beneficial to oneself as an individual but will also contribute to the betterment of the community in which one lives.

Generally speaking, altruism is the genuine source of benefit and happiness in this world. Thus if we were born in a realm of existence where the development of altruism was not possible, we would be in a rather hopeless situation, which is fortunately not the case. As human beings we have all the faculties appropriate for spiritual development, among them the most precious of all—the human brain. It is very important that we do not waste the great opportunity afforded by our being human, because time is a phenomenon that is momentary and does not wait. It is the nature of things that they go through a process of change and disintegration. Therefore, it is a matter of utmost importance that we make our human lives meaningful.

As explained earlier, just as one has a natural right to work for one's own happiness, so, in equal measure, do all sentient beings. What, then, is the difference between self and others? The only difference is that when one talks of one's own affairs, no matter how important one might be, one is only concerned with a single person, whereas the affairs of others concern the welfare of numberless living beings. The difference between the two concerns lies in the quantity.

Moreover, if one were totally unrelated to and independent of others, then one's indifference towards their welfare would be understandable, but this is not the case. All living beings survive in dependence upon others; even one's experiences of happiness and suffering come about in relation to one's interaction with others. One's dependence on others is not confined to day-to-day survival alone; all one's spiritual development depends upon others as well. It is only in relation to others that one can cultivate such human qualities as universal compassion, love, tolerance, generosity, etc. Even the Buddha's noble activities come about because there are other sentient beings to work for. If one thinks in such terms, one will find that working for one's own benefit, totally neglecting the welfare of others, is very selfish and hence unfair. When one compares the welfare of oneself with that of the numberless others, one finds that the welfare of others is far more important; and therefore giving up the benefits accruing to a single person for the sake of numberless others is a just and a righteous act. On the contrary, sacrificing the well-being of many for the benefit of one is not only a most unfair act but also a foolish one.

At this juncture, when we possess the intelligence to judge between right and wrong and also can draw inspiration from the examples of great *bodhisattvas* of the past, we should make every attempt to reverse our normal self-centered outlook. Our attitudes towards our own welfare should be such that we open ourselves completely to the service of others—so much so, that on our part there is not even a slight sense of possessiveness towards our belongings or our being. We have this great opportunity now.

We should rejoice in our fortune of having the precious chance, as humans, to practice altruism, a practice that I personally believe is the highest fulfillment of human value. I feel extremely fortunate to be able to speak on the importance and merits of a good heart and altruism. Should we persist in our normal self-centered tendencies and behavior in spite of our human birth, we would be wasting a great opportunity. Our tenure in this world should not be that of a troublemaker in the human community. Therefore, it is very important to realize the preciousness of the present opportunity and that such an opportunity comes about only through the aggregation of many favorable conditions.

On our part, as practitioners of dharma, it is very important to put the noble principles of the Buddhist doctrine into proper practice within our lives, and thus to experience the real fruits of the dharma. Dharma practitioners should set good examples and demonstrate the true value of the dharma. Otherwise, if our dharma remains only conceptual and is not tranformed into experience, its real value may not be realized.

The essence of dharma practice is to bring about a discipline within the mind, a state of mind free of hatred, lust and harmful intentions. Hence the entire message of the buddhadharma could be summed up in two succinct statements: "Help others," and "If you cannot help them, at least do not harm others." It is a grave error to think that apart from such a disciplining of the physical and mental faculties there is something else called "the practice of dharma." Various, and in some cases divergent, methods to achieve such an inner discipline have been taught in the scriptures by the Buddha.

This task of bringing about an inner discipline may look very complex and difficult at the outset, but if we really make the effort, we will see that it is not that complicated. We find ourselves caught in the confusion of all kinds of worldly con-

ceptions and negative emotions and so forth, but if we are able
to discover the right key through the practice of dharma, we
will be able to unravel this knot of confusion.

Practitioners of the dharma should have not only the ultimate aim of attaining full enlightenment, but also the goal of
becoming righteous and kind-hearted persons within this life
too. Let us say that there is a person attending this talk who
is normally very short-tempered, but as a result of his listening to the teachings and practicing the instructions he changes;
that really is the mark of having benefited from the dharma.
The fundamental questions, such as whether there is rebirth
or not, and whether or not full enlightenment is possible, are
difficult to answer. But what is very obvious to us is that a
positive state of mind and positive action lead to more happiness and peace, whereas their negative counterparts result in
undesirable consequences. Therefore, if as a result of our
dharma practice we are able to alleviate our sufferings and experience more happiness, that would in itself be a sufficient
fruit to encourage us further in our spiritual pursuits.

Even if we were not able to attain high spiritual realizations
in this lifetime, but were able to develop the altruistic mind
of *bodhicitta*—even to a very small degree—we would at least
be able to perceive all beings as our closest friends. If, on the
other hand, we were to cling to the self-cherishing attitude and
the misconception that grasps at the inherent existence of
things, there would be no possiblity of a genuine and lasting
mental peace and happiness, even if all the living beings around
us were trying to be friendly towards us. We can observe the
truth of this in our daily lives. The more altruism we develop
in a day, the more peaceful we find ourselves. Similarly, the
more self-centered we remain the more frustrations and trouble we encounter. All these reflections lead us to conclude that
a good heart and an altruistic motivation are indeed true sources
of happiness and are therefore genuine wish-granting jewels.

Now we are nearing the end of the twentieth century, an
era marked with revolution in many fields of human knowledge. During the eighteenth and nineteenth centuries, when

revolutionary scientific discoveries were being made, religion and science became more and more separated. Many people felt that they were perhaps incompatible. But in this century, when human intelligence has been so enriched by new knowledge derived through important scientific discoveries, a new trend is fortunately emerging. People in the scientific disciplines are taking a fresh interest in spiritual and moral concepts and are prepared to reappraise their attitudes towards the relevance of spiritual development in order to achieve a more complete view of life and the world. In particular, there is a growing interest among the scientific community in Buddhist philosophical thought. I am optimistic that over the next few decades there will be a great change in our world view both from the material and the spiritual perspectives.

2 Origin of Lamrim Instructions

This teaching on Lamrim (stages of the path) is one of eight great commentaries on Lamrim. This commentary explains the essential practices of Lamrim and also their preliminaries, in conjunction with the practice of *tantra*; specific parts of the meditations are associated with the tantric visualizations of nectar flowing within the body, and so forth. Among the eight commentaries, this text composed by Panchen Lama Choekyi Gyaltsen, called *Path to Bliss (Delam)*,[1] and also the commentary on it composed by Panchen Palden Yeshi and entitled *The Swift Path (Nyurlam)*,[2] are related to the practice of tantra, whereas the remaining six deal with Lamrim practices purely from a Perfection Vehicle standpoint.

For the practice of Lamrim, there are two major lineages, both stemming from Buddha Shakyamuni: the lineage of the Profound View transmitted through Manjushri, and the lineage of Vast Practice coming through Maitreya. These two lineages emerged as a result of an elucidation of the dual aspects of the subject matter of the Wisdom Sutras taught by the Buddha himself: the doctrine of emptiness (the explicit subject matter) and the stages of clear realization (the hidden meaning). Manjushri expounded the first and Maitreya the second.

Atisha integrated the two lineages, and from this integration there later arose the three lineages of the Kadam tradition. In Tibet, Atisha composed the text called *Jhangchup Lamgyi Dronme* (Lamp for the Path to Enlightenment), which served as the basis for many of the subsequent Lamrim treatises that emerged later in Tibet.

The great Lama Tsongkhapa, having received the three Kadam lineages, composed *Lamrim Chenmo* (The Great Exposition of the Stages of the Path), as well as an intermediate length version of it that omitted much elaboration but devoted special attention to the Two Truths in the section on special insight. He also wrote a very short form, in verse, called *Lamrim Nyamgur* (Songs of Spiritual Experience).

The Third Dalai Lama, Sonam Gyatso, composed a text called *Lamrim Sershunma* (Essence of Refined Gold), which is in fact a commentary on Lama Tsongkhapa's shortest version of Lamrim. The Fifth Dalai Lama composed a Lamrim, a commentary on the Third Dalai Lama's Lamrim, called *Jampel Shalung* (The Sacred Words of Manjushri), and Panchen Lama Choekyi Gyaltsen composed this Lamrim text, *Path to Bliss*. Panchen Palden Yeshi composed *The Swift Path* and then later Dagpo Ngawang Jamphel wrote a Lamrim in verse form. These eight are known as the eight great commentaries on the stages of the path.

Path to Bliss encompasses all the essential points of the sutra and tantra paths and has the advantage of having all the visualizations arranged in a manner conducive to systematic meditation. I know many people who have memorized this entire text and who undertake their practice on the basis of it, thus modeling the whole structure of the path on it.

I received the transmission of this Lamrim from the late Kyabje Trijang Rinpoche. Since the commentary being given is an experiential commentary, the tradition requires that I give the commentary four times,[3] which means three repetitions today and one more tomorrow.

Regarding the mode of teaching and studying such a text, it is important on the part of the teacher to have pure motivation, to have the altruistic intention to really benefit the disciples, and for the disciples on their part to always relate the teachings to their own minds, to have the altruistic intention to benefit all sentient beings, and to dedicate all the merit of the teaching for the benefit of others.

On your part, as disciples, you should conduct the appropriate visualizations. These should also be done with the preliminary practices. The preliminaries are explained here in terms of six preparatory practices, *Jorwai Choedrug*, often abbreviated as *Jorchoe*. The six preparatory practices are: (1) cleaning the meditation environment and arranging the images, scriptures, stupas—representations of the body, speech and mind of the Buddha—in their proper order; (2) beautifully setting up the offerings (which should be free from the taints of being procured through wrong means); (3) sitting on a comfortable meditation cushion in the seven-featured Vairocana posture, and, with the right state of mind, engaging in taking refuge and generating the altruistic motivation; (4) visualizing the merit field; (5) performing the seven-limbed practice and mandala offering, an endeavor encompassing all the essentials of purifying negativities and accumulating merit; and (6) beseeching the gurus to infuse one's mind with their inspirations.

One could do the preliminaries also on the basis of the guru yoga practice of *Lama Choepa*,[4] or a shorter version of the guru yoga practice known as *Gaden Lhagyama* (The Hundred Deities of the Joyous Land). It is not the ritual that is important—what is important is that one does the proper visualizations. The point is that you have to perform the visualizations that have been discussed by the teacher during the day. As the guru explains to you, your visualization should not be done in such a way that you have the notion that you are looking at something out there, but rather you should integrate the visualization with your own mind, trying to relate it to the state of your own mind, thus directly effecting some change and discipline within the mind. Undertaking a practice which combines contemplative and absorptive meditations on the basis of such a text and oral commentary constitutes receiving an experiential commentary. So the parts that the teacher covers daily should be visualized every day and the rest of the Lamrim practices could then be just reviewed. One could do that quite easily on the basis of some outlines, which is in fact much easier and also convenient. If you can, you should do that; if not, then there is nothing one can do about it.

It is important, when you are engaged in these practices, to focus your mind on them and not to let your mind be distracted, even by the arisal of other virtuous thoughts. You should not let your mind be led astray, but should rather channel it on the specific practice in which you are engaging, be it contemplative or absorptive. Letting your mind be distracted by thoughts that are totally unrelated to the practice that you have set out to undertake may actually give you a bad habit of letting your mind stray. So, right at the beginning of the session develop a strong determination that you shall never let your mind deviate from the practice. Furthermore, it is important to stick with the particular meditation that you have set out to undertake. Doing the practice properly, even for a short period of time, is better than spending a long time with all sorts of distractions. The emphasis should be on quality rather than quantity. You should also figure out means to overcome mental sinking and mental excitement, which may also depend on external factors like climate and food. The reason that we have not been able to make any progress at all, even in spite of our being acquainted with dharma for so long, is that we have not been able to focus our minds properly and pay the attention that is needed in such a practice. Therefore, I see the concentration of the mind when doing a practice as very important; if it is done, then there is every possibility that you will be able to undergo changes for the better.

Sometimes you might feel discouraged. Under such circumstances, it is important to compare your mind, your way of thinking and your actions of ten, fifteen or twenty years ago with the state of mind you have now. This will enable you to gain encouragement by seeing that you have made some progress. You will be able to notice a certain change in your mind: your interest in dharma is stronger, your faith is more firmly rooted, and you lose your temper less often. These are signs of making progress.

The full title of this text is *A Practical Guide to the Stages of the Path to Enlightenment: A Path to Bliss Leading to Omniscience*. The text is preceded by a salutation to one's own spiritual master who is seen as inseparable from the Buddha Vajradhara. Buddha Shakyamuni, the master of the sutra vehicle, appears in the aspect of Buddha Vajradhara, the master of tantric teachings. This text deals with all the essential points of both sutra and tantra; the form of the salutation accords also with this fact, because the success of the path, especially that of the tantric path, depends entirely upon receiving initial inspiration from a spiritual master.

It is very important, just as Lama Tsongkhapa pointed out in *Lamrim Chenmo*, to have proper reliance on a qualified spiritual master, because so much depends upon the master. For this reason, the practice of guru devotion is emphasized to a great degree at the beginning of this text. All the great traditions of Tibetan Buddhism emphasize the importance for serious meditators of having a very special guru devotion practice. When faith and conviction are taken as the basis for any of these practices—whether they be Mahamudra (Great Seal) or Lamrim—one will be able to make great spiritual progress. Many people have told me that they have experienced this for themselves.

Lord Buddha himself has outlined specific qualifications that a spiritual teacher must possess in relation to the different types of practices, in various scriptures on *vinaya*, *prajnaparamita*, and tantra. Lama Tsongkhapa, in his *Lamrim Chenmo*, has extensively discussed the qualifications of an ideal spiritual mentor.[5] Therefore, practitioners who are seeking a spiritual master have the information needed to judge whether or not the person in whom they are seeking spiritual guidance possesses the appropriate qualities. It is important to rely upon someone who will be able to show you the right path towards enlightenment. Once you have relied upon a master, it is important to maintain a proper reliance, in both thought and action.

Since this text explains the mode of doing the visualization of the Lamrim in a rather condensed form, the outlines are slightly different from those of *Lamrim Chenmo*. The outline of *Lamrim Chenmo* has four major divisions. These four are: (1) the exceptional qualities of the author, in order to demonstrate the authenticity of the teachings; (2) the exceptional qualities of the teaching, in order to inspire respect for the instructions; (3) the way in which the text possessing the two exceptional qualities should be studied and taught; and (4) the stages of leading disciples with the actual instructions.

In order for a dharma teaching or text to be considered authentic, its origins should be traceable to the original teachings of the Buddha himself. The instructions on Lamrim have their origin in the prajnaparamita sutras taught by the Buddha.

The root text of the Lamrim is regarded as being Maitreya's *Abhisamayalankara* (The Ornament of Clear Realizations), especially the section dealing with what is known as the "serial training" in the sixth chapter of the text. This work categorizes all the various stages of the spiritual journey to full enlightenment by a prospective bodhisattva into four trainings. These four are: (1) training in the complete aspects (*namzog jorwa*); (2) peak training (*tsemoi jorwa*); (3) serial training (*thargyi jorwa*); and (4) momentary training (*kechigmai jorwa*).[6] Basically, the summary verses at the end of the *Abhisamayalankara*, where the entire text is summarized into three divisions—the three objects of meditation, the four trainings, and the resultant *kayas* of buddhahood—are taken as the source of Lamrim meditations. There are specific verses also in the fourth chapter of that text where conviction and faith in the spiritual master are emphasized along with conviction in the law of causality. That section also outlines the process of cultivating the altruistic attitude, bodhicitta, and then engaging in the actual deeds, the practices of the six perfections—thus the entire practice of Lamrim.

There are actually various ways and means of undertaking a practice of dharma, suiting the diverse faculties, interests and needs of trainees. To study a text, we should take into account the circumstances, the situation, the time, the society and the community where a book was originally written or a teaching taught. For example, you will see a difference between the style and composition of commentaries and texts authored by the Indian masters and those authored by the Tibetan masters. We find that there are many variations in the styles and techniques adopted by different masters for leading disciples or trainees on the stages of the path. These diversities have a special significance.

The style and the process of the path as explained in the Lamrim were first initiated by the Indian master Atisha. Although he was Indian, since his text on the stages of the path was composed in Tibet, he took into account the mentality and needs of the Tibetan people and wrote a text that would lead the practitioners through the comprehensive yet condensed practices of the three scopes. Therefore, Lama Tsongkhapa, when commenting on the exceptional qualities of the author at the beginning of his *Lamrim Chenmo*, wrote down the qualifications of Atisha, thus implying that he was the actual author of the text. For the Tibetans, Atisha's kindness is indeed boundless.

Since the Gelug tradition later came to be known as the new Kadam tradition, retrospectively Atisha's tradition came to be known as the old Kadampa. The Kadam tradition that emerged from Atisha and his chief disciple Dromtonpa was really very impressive, very straightforward, practical and pure in its doctrine. Lama Tsongkhapa's various versions of Lamrim took Atisha's *Lamp* as their basis and complemented the section on special insight by adding materials from the major treatises of Indian masters such as Nagarjuna. In these sections, he not only explains the methods of cultivating the two factors of the path—wisdom and method—in a systematic way, but also clarifies many points that were left obscure before his time.

Then, as stated above, the First Panchen Lama composed this exceptional text on Lamrim. He was a great being with high realizations, and was totally non-sectarian, a person who was deeply admired by many great personalities of his time. As Lama Tsongkhapa mentioned in his *Lamrim Chenmo*, through the practice of Lamrim one could realize all the teachings of the Buddha as personal advice, see all his teachings as non-contradictory, and easily understand the ultimate intent of the Buddha. Thus, through such practice, the grave misdeed of abandoning the doctrine would be naturally prevented. Hence, one could say that the exceptional qualities of this text are: (1) an encompassing of the entire subject matter of Lamrim; (2) an easy applicability, as the text is composed in a style designed primarily for meditation; and (3) an endowment with the instructions of the two lineages. The text is quite condensed, yet very profound, consisting of all the essential points of Lamrim explained in conjunction with unique tantric visualizations.

For an intensive meditation on Lamrim practices it is essential to engage in a preliminary stage of practice, preparing for one's meditation not only a conducive external environment but also a receptive mind. This can best be undertaken within the framework of what are known as the six preparatory practices.

PART II:
PREPARATORY PRACTICES

1 Creating a Conducive Environment

First, you should seek a proper environment and arrange a comfortable seat, slightly upraised at the rear so that when you do long meditation sessions you will not feel tired. Then, the position of your body should be maintained in the Vairocana posture: your legs crossed, if possible; your spine straight; your head slightly bent and the eyes downcast, looking in front of you; and the tip of the tongue touching the palate of the mouth. You should judge for yourself the best position for your eyes: some people find that doing the meditations with open eyes is much more powerful, whereas others find it very distracting. For them, slightly closing the eyes might prove more beneficial. Generally speaking, I think that visualizations of the deities and so forth, if conducted with the eyes open, will have a greater clarity. Sometimes it may also be beneficial to just sit down facing a wall directly, so that you don't have any distraction. The point is that you should figure out a way that you find least distracting and that permits you greatest clarity.

You may find the position uncomfortable. If so, at the beginning of your meditation—just as a symbol, a sign of auspiciousness—try to sit cross-legged at least for a while and then later you can adopt leg postures more comfortable for you.

Place the hands in the position of meditative equipoise, four finger-widths below your navel, the right palm on top of the left, the two thumbs touching each other, forming a triangle there. You should keep your elbows away from your body, slightly outstretched so that air can pass through. Keeping the upper tip of the tongue touching the palate of the mouth may prevent thirst; otherwise, if you just open your mouth, then—as a result of breathing meditations and so forth—you might feel thirsty.

The most important thing is to have an object appropriate to your meditation. To help you have a better visualization, it is good to have a representation of the deity on whom you are meditating, such as the Buddha Shakyamuni, the master of the doctrine, and to look at it frequently. If you don't have any representations, that is all right, but if you do have them, they should be arranged properly—statues, scriptures, and so forth.

I always make the remark that inside Tibet, since the Chinese have meted out great destruction of religious monuments, making statues is quite important, because they can be used to point out to the younger generation that such is the Buddha, and such is Avalokiteshvara, the patron deity of Tibet and the embodiment of compassion, and such is Manjushri, the deity of wisdom, and so on. But here, representations— for a serious practitioner—are not indispensable. Many masters of the past, such as the great meditator Milarepa, achieved high realizations without depending on these external factors. It is important to be able to judge what are the most essential elements.

Furthermore, I often mention that although there have been very great masters in Tibet who have had high realizations, at the same time there have been many shortcomings in Tibet as well. Even in religious practices worldly considerations have crept in, so it is very important for all practitioners to realize that the practice of dharma means bringing about a discipline within one's mind—in other words, training the mind.

Therefore, one should not view one's dharma practice as being something decorative, regarding statues and images as material possessions or as furnishings for one's house, or thinking that because there is an empty space on a wall one might as well put up a thangka for decoration. That kind of attitude should not be cultivated. When you arrange the statues or thangkas, you should do so out of a deep respect from the mind, moved by your faith and conviction. If you can arrange these physical representations—statues and so forth—out of deep respect and faith, that's all right. On the other hand, the attitude that they are merely material possessions is dangerous and destructive. I think that some people who have a cupboard or the like in which they keep all their precious possessions may arrange an altar on it just for the sake of decoration. This is very wrong.

It is also dangerous to arrange statues of very wrathful *dharmapalas*, or protectors, without also having a statue of Buddha Shakyamuni. One's attitude in arranging such statues, if it is influenced by worldly considerations, such as thinking that if one propitiates such and such a protector one's wealth will be increased and so forth, is unsafe. Sometimes I feel it is almost like entrusting these deities on the altar on top of the cupboard to protect the things that are inside the cupboard and perhaps increase them if possible! Such an outlook is contradictory to the practice of dharma. If the great Kadampa masters such as Dromtonpa were to come in person and see such an arrangement made with such motivation, they would never admire or be pleased by it, but would denounce it. I can guarantee such a response.

Having such motivations is not the proper way to become a Buddhist; the proper way to become a Buddhist is to bring about some positive change within the mind. Any practice that can give you more courage when you are undergoing a very difficult time and that can provide you with some kind of solace and calmness of mind is a true practice of the dharma.

I thought that it would be more beneficial if I explained the disadvantages of arranging the altar in such a manner and with the wrong motivation, than if I explained the advantages of properly arranging an altar. If we were to spend all our energy and time simply on the arrangement of beautiful altars and so forth, totally neglecting the development of the mind, then that would be very bad.

The environment where you are doing the meditation should be properly cleaned. While cleaning, you should cultivate the motivation that since you are engaged in the task of accumulating great stores of merit by inviting the hosts of buddhas and bodhisattvas to this environment, it is important to have a clean place. You should see that all the external dirt and dust around you is basically a manifestation of the faults and stains within your own mind. You should see that the most important aim is to purge these stains and faults from within your mind. Therefore, as you cleanse the environment, think that you are also purifying your mind. Develop the very strong thought that by cleaning this place you are inviting the host of buddhas and bodhisattvas who are the most supreme merit field, and that you will subsequently engage in a path that will enable you to purge your mind of the stains of delusions.

Then, if you have a representation of the Buddha's speech, such as a text on Lamrim, *The Perfection of Wisdom in Eight Thousand Verses*, or any other texts, it would be good to arrange them properly. Offerings can also be arranged, if you have some—but if you do not have them, they can be done without. When you make offerings, it is important to see that the materials of the offerings have not been wrongly procured. There is nothing to be admired about elaborate offerings if the materials for the offerings are obtained in a wrong way, because the negativities accumulated in the process of procuring such materials will not be offset by the merits gained through offering them. So, such offerings are pointless and foolish. However, a great store of merit can be gained on the basis of making offerings properly.

2 Preparing the Mind

One's motivation at the beginning is very important, because whether or not one's practice becomes successful and effective depends upon the initial motive and attitude. For the development of the right attitude, the practice of refuge and the generation of bodhicitta are vital. Through the practice of the two one should be able to bring about some discipline and transformation within one's mind.

So, on a comfortable meditation seat you should adopt the right physical posture and then generate the appropriate motivation. After you are seated facing eastwards (or imagining that you are facing eastwards), reflect that you are very fortunate to have this opportunity to engage in the practice of dharma, and that you will make this session most worthwhile. Rejoice that you have this opportunity, and think that, at this juncture, when you have obtained most of the important conditions for making progress on the path, there is hope that you can embark on the right path and make some spiritual progress.

It is almost like being at a critical crossroad and taking a new turn in your journey, embarking on a path leading to the achievement of the omniscient state—not for your own sake alone, but rather for the benefit of all living beings.

Also reflect that you possess within yourself, as do all living beings, the potential or the seed of buddhahood, and also have access to the means by which this potential can be successfully activated. Think: I shall explore this potentiality to its fullest extent, and I shall make the most of the present opportunity. Furthermore, you should reflect upon the fact that you have been extremely fortunate to have received many teachings from the masters and that you are equipped with the knowledge to undertake the practice properly.

You should understand that the whole purpose of listening to teachings, taking teachings and studying them is to put them into practice, just as after having learned how to prepare a certain dish, you utilize that knowledge to make the dish and derive full nutritional benefit from it. What you know should be put into practice immediately; you can thus derive the benefit of having some transformation within your mind. Even though it might be a very minor effort, a very small practice just leaving imprints within your mind, still you must think that it is worthwhile to do. Otherwise, your knowledge of dharma will be quite fruitless, and like merely playing something on a tape.

At the initial stage it is important to have short sessions, as many of them as possible in a day. Generally speaking, the texts speak of four sessions, two in the morning and two in the afternoon, but you could make it into six. The length and the number of the sessions should be judged according to your own personal disposition. Your practice should be enduring, and you should undertake it with sustained effort. But because at the initial stage much depends upon your physical condition—the body's influence on the mind is very powerful—you have to take the body's condition into account. So it is very important to be careful. Some practitioners who put the body to a severe test in their practice of dharma may end up losing it, as such an act is very destructive.

Once you have made good progress on the spiritual path, you will gradually gain control over your body and mind through meditative stabilization. Particularly when you have gained control over the subtle energies, you will be able to employ your body for any length of time without there being any danger of imbalances being caused by your spiritual practices. This stage is quite difficult to attain; therefore at the initial stage it is very important to be cautious and very skillful.

I make this remark for the people who are undertaking the practice of dharma very seriously as solitary meditators in the mountains. For you, it is crucial right from the beginning to be skillful and cautious so that you can maintain a sustained effort. If you can undertake such a practice when you are young, you will be able to make great progress, whereas if you start when you are already too old, you may not be able to make much progress.

You can do the sessions at the initial stage for about half an hour or maybe an hour, depending upon your own conditions, and after that you can end the session and do other practices or take a rest.

For those of you who are not able to devote all your time to meditation, there is nevertheless the possibility of engaging in practice in a serious way. For example, the students at the monastic universities in South India can, with some effort, do meditations during the prayers. When you recite the prayers, you can mentally do the contemplation. The lifestyle and daily routine at these monasteries have been structured by the great masters of the past in a way that is most conducive to individual practice as well as to the flourishing of the dharma.

If you find that your mind is in a very fluctuating emotional state—displaying anger, hatred, attachment and so forth—then you should first try to calm down that state of strong emotion. This should be done by first transforming it into a neutral state of mind, because there is no way that one can switch directly from a negative state of mind to a positive one. Therefore, you should first reduce the force of these emotions and fluctuations and try to bring about some sort of calmness, using any means—such as taking a stroll or concentrating on the inhalation and exhalation of the breath—that will enable you to forget what you are immediately feeling. This will help you to reduce the force of strong emotion, thereby giving you the calmness necessary for the practice of dharma. Like a white piece of cloth which could be dyed any color that you desire, such a neutral state of mind could then be transformed into a virtuous state of mind.

You could also engage in the preliminary practices of performing 100,000 prostrations, recitations of the Vajrasattva mantra, and so forth. When you undertake these practices, you should do them properly, not being only concerned about the number. Many great masters of the past of all traditions have emphasized the importance of these preliminary practices—they will enable you to have a very firm start. If through them you can acquire a fertile mind, then when the seed of meditation is planted, it will readily bear the fruits of realizations.

Having successfully neutralized the emotional fluctuations within your mind and having restored a reasonable degree of calmness, you should then engage in the practice of taking refuge and generating the altruistic aspiration to attain full enlightenment. Taking refuge in the Three Jewels is the factor that distinguishes one's practice from that of an erroneous path, and the generation of the altruistic mind makes it superior to the paths aiming at individual liberation.

TAKING THE PRELIMINARY REFUGE

First of all, visualize the objects of refuge. This should be done by visualizing, above and in front of you in space, your own spiritual master in the aspect of Buddha Shakyamuni. His hands are in the normal position, the left arm in a meditative posture, holding a bowl full of nectar symbolizing victory over death and all forms of obstruction, the right in the gesture of touching the ground, signifying his victory over the divine youth mara.[7]

Visualizing one's own root guru as the object of refuge allows one swiftly to obtain inspiration; visualizing him in the aspect of Buddha Shakyamuni makes such an inspiration more extensive and vast. Thus you should visualize the spiritual teacher in the form of Buddha Shakyamuni, possessing all the major and minor noble marks of the Buddha such as the crown protrusion, in the nature of light, crystal clear, very radiant. This clarity symbolizes the union of the illusory body and Clear Light.[8]

The guru is seated in the *vajrasana* cross-legged position. This position of the legs symbolizes the Buddha's having realized the completely enlightened state through the four vajrasanas (inseparable crossings): the *asanas* of the legs, the channels, the energy winds, and the vital drops. This position further symbolizes invulnerability to any form of obstacle.

Your spiritual master in the form of Buddha Shakyamuni is seated in the center of a very vast and expansive throne, surrounded by four small thrones, on a variegated lotus and sun and moon disks. In front of him, on a small throne, is your own root guru who is kind to you in all three ways, the guru to whom you feel most close. You should visualize him in his normal appearance, excepting any physical defects he may have. Then visualize him being surrounded by all the gurus from whom you have taken teachings directly.

I found that some commentaries state that even though your root guru may be a lay person, when you visualize him in the merit field you should see him in the aspect of an ordained bhikshu.

On Shakyamuni's left imagine Manjushri surrounded by the lineage masters of the Profound View, on his right Maitreya surrounded by the lineage masters of the Vast Practice, at the rear Vajradhara surrounded by the lineage masters of the Experiential Practice. These lineage masters form what is known as the "five groups of lamas."

All of them are surrounded by the meditational deities of the four classes of tantra, bodhisattvas, *arhats*, heroes, heroines, and protectors. There are different ways of visualizing the heroes and heroines: heroes on the right and heroines on the left, or, in some traditions, heroes and heroines in union.

For us, what is of prime importance at the beginning is to develop a deep conviction in the Three Jewels in general, and in particular, the possibility of achieving dharma, Buddha and *sangha* within ourselves. If we do not develop this conviction, we will not have a very firm and stable foundation. Without such a conviction, if we complement our practice with various visualizations of dharmapalas, heroes, heroines and so forth, instead of benefiting us, this diversity might actually harm and confuse.

For this reason it is most important to have a very clear understanding of the Three Jewels. This in turn requires an understanding of the dharma, which requires an understanding of what is called the truth of cessation, which requires a good understanding of profound emptiness.

So, first of all you should have the deep conviction that cessation of the sufferings and the delusions is possible, and also that it is possible within your mind. True cessation is a state where you have destroyed the delusions at their root so that there remains no potential for their re-emergence. Such a cessation can be realized only through the true paths that penetrate into the nature of reality.

When you develop this conviction, you will also be able to develop faith in a being who has really mastered cessation, who is the Buddha—a person who has fully accomplished the realization of the dharma. If you contemplate along such lines, you will be able to develop a very deep faith and conviction in Buddha Shakyamuni and see him as an incomparable master.

What distinguishes Buddhist practitioners from others is the factor of taking refuge. But merely seeking a refuge out of the fear of suffering is not unique to Buddhists; non-Buddhists could also have such a motivation. The unique practice of refuge that Buddhists should have is that of taking refuge in the Buddha out of a deep conviction in his exceptional qualities and realizations. If you think in such terms you will be able to understand Lama Tsongkhapa's profound praise of Buddha Shakyamuni: "Those who are far from his doctrine always reinforce the illusion of self-existence that they have within themselves, whereas those who follow his guidance will be able to free themselves from such confusions."

The conviction that cessation of suffering is possible will furthermore enable you to develop deep faith and conviction in the sangha, the spiritual community that will provide you with companionship on your path. If you develop this proper understanding of the Three Jewels, you will have developed a good understanding of the general framework of the entire Buddhist path. Only then will you be able to understand the particular significance of various visualizations, such as those of meditational deities, heroes, heroines, protectors, bodhisattvas, arhats and so forth, because then you will see the importance of their differing appearances.

Just as Sakya Pandita said in his *Domsum Rabye* (The Divisions of the Three Vows), unless one develops a good understanding of the Three Jewels, one will not understand the significance of the protectors and so forth. I have a German friend who is quite familiar with the Buddha's teachings; when she visited monasteries in the Himalayan regions, some people pointed out to her that protectors and meditational deities are superior to Buddha Shakyamuni. My friend told me that she didn't find that assertion to be very convincing. She is right, because if you do not have a proper understanding of the Three Jewels, then when you see all these different images, you will have the notion that they are totally different from, and unrelated to, each other, as though they were inherently existent, thus giving you a misunderstanding of their relationships to each other.

Therefore, I think that if you base your knowledge of Buddhism on a proper understanding of the Three Jewels, which is a common foundation for Buddhist practice, then your understanding of the meditational deities will be good. Then you will also understand the importance of the different kayas, the various bodies of the Buddha,[9] and the importance of the path that has the aspect of union of method and wisdom. Only at that point will you be able to understand the significance and importance of these meditational deities that are the physical manifestation of the union of method and wisdom. Without the proper understanding of the Three Jewels and the general framework of the Buddhist path, if you simply visualize a very impressive and wrathful-looking deity, your practice, instead of being beneficial, may turn out to be quite harmful and may increase anger and emotion.

If you find such complex visualizations quite difficult at the initial stage and disturbing to your main practice of taking refuge and generating the mind of enlightenment (bodhicitta), then a shorter version of visualizing the Three Jewels may be more suitable—that is, visualizing your spiritual master alone, but seeing him as the embodiment of the entire merit field. Visualize him in the aspect of Buddha Shakyamuni and perceive him as the embodiment of the Buddha, dharma, and sangha. This simpler practice is known as the Jewel Embodiment (*Kuntu Norbu Lug*). For some people, the visualization of many different figures in a merit field is more beneficial and effective, but for others the visualization of just a single figure alone, such as the Buddha Shakyamuni or your own spiritual master in the Buddha's form, may prove more effective and powerful.

Whether to undertake a very extensive visualization or to use a short and condensed visualization is a matter that you yourself should decide on the basis of your own mental attitude and disposition. The point is, whatever is more beneficial and effective for you should be adopted, since the purpose of all this visualization is to bring about some effect and change and progress within your mind. So, if you can achieve these with a condensed form of visualization, that's fine, and if you think you need a more elaborate version, choose that.

If you want to do the practice of taking refuge in a more elaborate way, then—just as you find described in the first chapter of *Abhisamayalankara*—begin by reflecting upon the ultimate nature of all phenomena that makes it possible for them to function on the conventional level. All these phenomena have dual aspects, the ultimate nature which is the empty nature, and then, on the conventional level, their individual appearances and various characteristics such as production, disintegration and so forth. Reflect on these dual aspects, the Two

Truths of phenomena, and then elaborate these Two Truths further and reflect upon the Four Noble Truths. Although all phenomena lack inherent existence, when they appear to us they appear as if they had an inherent nature and existed in and of themselves. It is ignorance that grasps at the belief in the true existence of phenomena and serves as the root cause of all subsequent delusions. Once we realize that ignorant mind states are deceptive and distorted, we will be able to see through their illusions and be able to free ourselves of ignorance, thus enabling us to achieve the state of cessation.

Generally speaking, when we talk of refuge we are referring to different types of refuge: outer, the practice of refuge that is common to the lesser vehicle; inner, the unique refuge of Mahayana; and secret, the unique refuge of tantra.[10] This latter refers to the practice of going for refuge to the meditational deities, heroes, heroines, etc., which also has its own division into outer, inner and secret refuges. We find that the practice of refuge is very important as well as vast, and that it should conform to the kind of practice we are undertaking.

Having visualized the objects of refuge, imagine in front of them the scriptures composed by great beings, in the aspects of texts and in their nature created of light. These scriptures should be imagined also as resounding with the sounds of the letters as though they were being read.

All the objects of the merit field should be seen as looking pleasantly at you. Different commentaries explain the reason for the merit fields gazing at us with pleasure as follows: Although our own states of mind are very weak and inferior, and therefore there are no grounds for the merit fields to be delighted with us, since we are now embarking on a path that will lead us to a spiritual transformation, we imagine that in order to encourage us in our initiative the merit fields gaze at us with delight. This explanation is according to the tradition of the late Kyabje Trijang Rinpoche. Another tradition maintains that the significance of this visualization is that these noble beings display such a gesture in order to give us more courage and determination. On your part, you should cultivate deep respect for and faith in the members of the merit field by reflecting on their great qualities and kindness.

After having visualized the merit fields, reflect upon the fact that you have experienced intense sufferings over infinite lifetimes, and that if you pursue your present state of mind and action, you will continue to torment yourself with sufferings in the cycle of existence. Therefore, right now determine that you shall engage in the practice that will bring about some change, and will undertake this practice of taking refuge in the Buddha, dharma, and sangha as well as in the guru.

With such reflections, repeat the refuge formula:

> I go for refuge to the Guru.
> I go for refuge to the Buddha.
> I go for refuge to the Dharma.
> I go for refuge to the Sangha.

While doing this recitation, visualize yourself surrounded by all the mother sentient beings in their human aspect. This is done because human beings possess the highest potential for making spiritual progress. Other masters explain that all these sentient beings, although visualized in the aspect of human beings, should be thought of in the nature of their individual forms of existence and actively undergoing the sufferings of their particular realms.

When you recite the refuge formula, imagine that you do so in unison with all these sentient beings around you. Imagine that all of you possess the basic factors of fear of the sufferings in this cycle of existence and the conviction that the three objects of refuge have the power and capacity to help free you from this fear. Whether or not your practice of refuge is successful depends upon whether or not you have the right attitude, these basic factors. So, equipped with these two factors—fear of cyclic existence and deep conviction in the three objects of refuge—if you repeat the refuge formula as much as possible, your practice of refuge will be successful. On the other hand, if you are not equipped with the two basic factors, even though you might repeat the refuge formula many times, you won't make much progress.

You should also reflect upon the acute sufferings of all the sentient beings around you, the general sufferings of cyclic existence, and the specific sufferings of the individual states of existence. Sentient beings like yourself, human beings, although not actively undergoing the acute sufferings of hell realms and animal realms, are nevertheless in the process of aggregating conditions for such sufferings in the future because they are actively working for their own downfall. Therefore, it is only a matter of time until you actually experience such sufferings. By reflecting upon the sufferings of cyclic existence, you should develop fear of them; this should immediately be followed by a deep conviction that the Three Jewels have the power and capacity to relieve you from such sufferings.

Among the Three Jewels, the actual refuge is the dharma, because it is only by bringing about the realization of dharma within yourself that you will be able to free yourself and relieve yourself from the sufferings of cyclic existence. Therefore, dharma is the actual refuge, and the Buddha is the master who shows you the path leading to realization, and the sangha is the spiritual community that provides you with companionship on your path. Thus, these Three Jewels have the potential and power to relieve you from the cycle of existence, but you should not have the attitude that those who entrust themselves to them are automatically relieved without the need for practical initiative on their own parts.

So that your taking of refuge accords with your basic ideals as a practitioner of the bodhisattva path, you should complement your practice of refuge with the generation of a deep compassion towards all beings. You should think that not only yourself but all other sentient beings revolve in this cycle of existence fraught with misery and suffering; although they seek happiness and wish to avoid suffering, still they have to undergo this fate, against their wishes.

So, equipped with these three factors—the fear of cyclic existence, the conviction that the Three Jewels have the power to relieve you, and a genuine sense of compassion for the sufferings of all other sentient beings—then, as a physical expression of your sense of the unbearableness of the sufferings of cyclic existence for yourself and other sentient beings, you should recite the refuge formula. The recitation is an expression of what you feel inside, one that is spontaneous and natural. It is only when you have very strong anxiety and emotion that your cry of anguish comes out spontaneously and naturally.

It is important that the meaning of the verses should be integrated into your own mind. If you merely recite the verses with a distracted mind, you might accumulate certain virtues of reciting religious teachings, but you will not be able to derive much benefit.

You should do the repetition with the hands folded, taking refuge in the guru as many times as possible. When you do the repetition, visualize the five groups of gurus, focusing upon them especially and thinking that all the negativities that are committed in relation to these gurus, and particularly the Three Jewels, are being purified. To do this, visualize nectars of five colors descending from the bodies of these gurus; the nectars enter your body and purify your mind of all the negativities committed in relation to the Three Jewels and particularly your own spiritual root guru. You receive the inspiration of body, speech, and mind of all the gurus, particularly your own spiritual master. Then imagine that you are now placed under the kind care of the spiritual master. These three visualizations—purifying the negativities, receiving the inspirations from the objects of refuge, and finally being placed under the kind care of these refuges—are vital.

The three phases of visualization should be done when you take refuge in the Buddha, dharma, and sangha. Generally speaking, you should not have the notion that there is a separate guru from the Buddha. A qualified guru should be a buddha possessing all the great qualities of the Buddha. Therefore, there isn't any being called *guru* apart from the Three Jewels, particularly in the context of Mahayana practice and especially that of the tantric path, because in all these practices all realizations depend upon receiving the right inspiration from the spiritual master. Particularly in the practice of tantra, one takes vows and pledges from the guru, seeing him as inseparable from the principal deity of a mandala. Therefore, receiving a transmission from a living person becomes an extremely important element in the practice of tantra. This point is demonstrated by the simple fact that although in the Perfection Vehicle practice the bodhicitta vow can be obtained from a representation of the refuge, such as a statue, tantric vows can be received only from a living person.

Although you do not have the opportunity and fortune to have direct access to Buddha Vajradhara himself, you do have access to the inspiration that comes from him in an uninterrupted lineage. Because it is the guru who transmits this uninterrupted lineage to you, he is the link between you and Vajradhara. Therefore, he is regarded as the only entrance through which you receive the inspirations of the Buddha. Because of the extremely vital role that the guru plays in your spiritual development, a specific refuge is taken in the guru.

Light rays emanate from the hearts of the spiritual masters of the five groups. Visualize these light rays in the form of straws of light that enter through the crown protrusions of yourself and all sentient beings. Through these flow streams of nectar; thus you purify the negativities that you have committed in relation to the Three Jewels and receive all their inspiration of body, speech, and mind. You should imagine, as a result, that you are placed under the kind care of the Three Jewels and particularly of the spiritual master. This practice of taking refuge should be followed by the generation of bodhicitta.

PRELIMINARY GENERATION OF BODHICITTA

The etymological meaning of the Tibetan term for bodhicitta, *sem kye*, is "to enhance one's courage or mental attitude." Therefore, bodhicitta is an altruistic state of mind that aspires to attain the completely enlightened state for the benefit of all other sentient beings.

In order to generate such a powerful altruistic mind, it is important to focus upon all the sentient beings around you and realize the fact that, like yourself, they have the wish to achieve happiness and avoid suffering. You should think: I can help them fully only when I myself have achieved the completely enlightened state, the noble state that the objects of refuge in front of me have all realized, for the benefit of all sentient beings.

The actual generation of the altruistic mind is done by reciting the following formula:

> I go for refuge until I am enlightened
> To the Buddha, the Dharma and the highest Assembly.
> From the virtuous merit that I collect
> By practicing giving and other perfections,
> May I attain Buddhahood
> To be able to benefit all beings.

Recite this verse three times, seven times, or as many times as possible. While reciting, do the visualization of generating bodhicitta as powerfully as possible, so as to lead you to the conviction that without achieving the completely enlightened state, you will not be able to help all other sentient beings.

With such a genuine and strong attitude, you should imagine that, due to the force of such generation of the mind, Buddha Shakyamuni in front of you is pleased, and a replica of him emerges, comes to the crown of your head, and dissolves into you through your crown aperture. Your body, speech, and mind become inseparable from those of the Buddha. Then you dissolve into emptiness; at that point meditate on emptiness and from within it arise into Buddha Shakyamuni, sitting on a throne upraised by lions. Imagine that you have achieved the resultant state that you were aspiring to achieve.

Alternatively, you may imagine replicas—in the form of light rays—of the Three Jewels, particularly your spiritual master, entering through your crown and dissolving into you, whereby you yourself dissolve into emptiness. From within emptiness, you arise in the aspect of the enlightened being that you have been seeking, that is, as the Buddha endowed with all his exceptional qualities. Imagine that you have turned yourself into such a being, and then emanate infinite light rays around you to all sentient beings, transforming them into Buddha Shakyamunis. Rejoice, thinking that you have been able to fulfill your aim of working for the benefit of all beings.

This practice could also be done in conjunction with the visualizations of tantric deity yoga as well. Visualize that due to your intensive practice the gurus are delighted and the force of their appreciation causes them to dissolve into you through your crown aperture. The merging of your guru with you now causes you to gradually dissolve from above and below into the Clear Light of emptiness. This kind of visualization should be performed only by practitioners who have been initiated into tantra.

At this point it is effective to reflect upon emptiness, thinking, Who is the being that has dissolved into me, and who am I? By contemplating on the five-point analysis[11] as outlined in *Tsawa Sherab* (The Root Wisdom) by Nagarjuna, reflect upon the fact that "I" is a mere imputation on the basis of the physical and mental aggregates. There is no inherently existent guru apart from the self, that is a mere label imputed upon his physical and mental aggregates. Therefore, we will find that the spiritual master in whom we entrust ourselves and in whom we take refuge, himself lacks an inherently existent nature.

Similarly, for we who take refuge in him, there is no inherently existent self in the sense of a self that is the master of the physical and mental aggregates and is totally distinct and separate from them. Thus, you will be able to understand the lack of inherent existence or, in other words, the emptiness of the self. This reflection on emptiness will enable you to dissolve yourself—in imagination—into emptiness, from which you arise into Buddha Shakyamuni as described above. The practice of complementing compassion and love with wisdom realizing emptiness is very effective, particularly the reflection upon the ultimate nature of your own mind and on the fact that the buddha-potential is inherent in all sentient beings— the essential nature of your own mind is pure and never polluted by delusions. Delusion has never penetrated into the core of the essential nature of the mind; therefore, delusions are adventitious.

THE FOUR IMMEASURABLES

Your generation of bodhicitta, the altruistic aspiration to attain enlightenment for the benefit of others, should then be complemented with the practice of the four immeasurables: love, compassion, joy, and equanimity. These are factors that will give great impetus to your realization of the altruistic mind and will also greatly enhance it.

To do this practice, think that although you are very fortunate to be doing this visualization of turning into a buddha, you do so only in the imagination, and you yourself are still an ordinary being. Then you should try to discover what prevents you from truly becoming a buddha, and you will find that it is that your mind is under the influence of fluctuating emotions towards friends and enemies. In order to overcome these, you should practice love, equanimity, and so forth.

With such reflections, recite the following three or seven times:

As much as I wish that all beings be free of partiality such as emotional closeness and distance induced by attachment and hatred, may they abide in equanimity. I, myself, will endeavor to make this become a reality. O Guru-deity, empower me with your inspiring strength to fulfill this aspiration.

As much as I wish that all beings be endowed with happiness and its causes, may they achieve them. I, myself, will endeavor to make this become a reality. O Guru-deity, empower me with your inspiring strength to fulfill this aspiration.

As much as I wish that all beings be free of suffering and its causes, may they be relieved of them. I, myself, will endeavor to make this become a reality. O Guru-deity, empower me with your inspiring strength to fulfill this aspiration.

As much as I wish that all beings never be separated from the excellent joy of favorable migrations and liberation from the cycle of existence, may they achieve this. I, myself, will endeavor to make this become a reality. O Guru-deity, empower me with your inspiring strength to fulfill this aspiration.

EXCEPTIONAL BODHICITTA

Next, you should generate what is called exceptional bodhicitta, a very strong and powerful form of bodhicitta that cannot be cultivated by practitioners of little courage. Therefore, the practitioners of this Lamrim should have in their generation of bodhicitta a strong sense of urgency, that of working to achieve the completely enlightened state within a short period of time—one lifetime. The text uses the phrase "quickly, quickly"; the first *quickly* refers to the achievement of the completely enlightened state within one lifetime, and the second refers to its achievement within three years. However, such a note of anxiety or urgency has its dangers, as it might actually lead to one's disappointment and discouragement when one doesn't find any realization as a result of practice, even after a long period of time.

Say to yourself, "To achieve the completely enlightened state within the shortest time, I shall engage in the profound path of guru deity yoga." You should develop the conviction that all the buddhas, bodhisattvas, and meditational deities are various aspects and appearances of your own guru. You should be able to see your own spiritual master as the embodiment of all the Three Jewels: his mind as the Buddha, his speech as the dharma, and his body as the sangha. In short, you should undertake the practice of such a yoga on the basis of viewing your own mind inseparably from the guru, the Three Jewels, the meditational deity and so forth. So, here the preliminary practice of Lamrim is taken in conjunction with the guru yoga practice of tantra.

3 Visualization of the Merit Field

Now visualize in front of you, as explained during the practice of refuge, your spiritual master above in space in the aspect of Buddha Shakyamuni. In front of him is your master in his normal appearance, surrounded by the gurus from whom you have received teachings directly. On his right are the lineage masters of the Vast Practice, on his left those of the Profound View, and in the rear those of the Experiential Lineage.[12] All of these groups are surrounded by meditational deities, buddhas, bodhisattvas, heroes, heroines and so forth.

Visualize the crown, throat, heart, navel and secret regions of all the members of the merit field marked by the syllables OM, AH, HUM, SVA and HA respectively. These syllables are the seeds of the five dhyani buddhas[13] and represent the body, speech, mind, actions and virtues of all the buddhas.

Light rays emanate from the syllable HA at the heart of the Guru Buddha Shakyamuni, inviting wisdom beings[14] identical to the ones you have visualized; a complete set of the merit field invited wisdom beings dissolves into each and every individual figure of the merit field, so that you can perceive each figure of the merit field as an embodiment of the entire refuge. Doing this also enables you to see each of them as a manifestation of your own spiritual master. It is through his kindness and in order to tame us that he has manifested in all these various forms; seeing things this way will help you to develop more faith in your guru. Meditation on a merit field of such a scale has a great significance.

For some people, however, the Jewel Embodiment practice, visualization of a single spiritual master, one's own root guru, may be more effective.

One could also do the visualization of the merit field as explained in *Lama Choepa* guru yoga practice,[15] which is the visualization that one finds in the six preparatory practices. It is meant for practitioners who have received initiation and who undertake this practice in conjunction with highest yoga tantra. Those who have not received any tantric initiations should not do the visualization of the merit field as explained in *Jorchoe Kelsang Dringyen*, because in that text the figures of the merit field are generated from the wisdom of bliss and emptiness, and if you have not received any initiation at all and have not cultivated this wisdom within you—even in simulation—it is impossible to borrow that wisdom from the merit field.

So, do the visualization of the merit field as suits your own mental disposition and then, focused upon it, engage in the practice of accumulating merit. This is done on the basis of the seven-limbed practice.

4 *Seven-Limbed Practice*

The seven parts of the practice are encompassed by two practices—the purification of negativities and the enhancing of the store of merit. When you engage in the practice, it is very important to understand that each and every one of the seven limbs[16] has its individual purpose and significance, and only with such knowledge can you engage properly in the practice. The seven limbs are: prostration, offering, confession, rejoicing, requesting to turn the wheel of the dharma, entreating not to enter into nirvana, and dedication of merit.

When you recite the verses of the seven-limbed practice, it is important to fold your palms to demonstrate the physical expression of the prostration. You should not feel embarrassed about folding the hands when reciting the prayers. A sense of shame and embarrassment should accompany only an indulgence in negative actions, when your conscience should be able to guard you well. On the contrary, people often demonstrate feelings of heroism and pleasure when indulging in such actions, which is very sad.

VERSES OF THE SEVEN-LIMBED PRAYER

1   Prostration

> To my lama, who embodies all Buddhas
> Who in nature is Vajradhara, and
> Who is the root of the Three Jewels,
> Ah, to my Lama I bow down.

> To all-compassionate Buddha Vajradhara,
> To perfect seers Tilopa and Naropa,
> The glorious Dombipa and Atisha:
> To the tantric practice lineage I bow down.

> To Maitreya, Asanga, Vasubhandu, Vimuktisena,
> Paramasena, Vinitasena, Shrikirti, Singhabadra,
> Kusali the Second, and Dharmakirti of the Golden
>   Isles:
> To the lineage of bodhimind's vast action I bow down.

> To Manjushri, destroyer of grasping at "is" and "is
>   not,"
> And to Nagarjuna, Chandrakirti, Vidyakokila the
>   Great,
> Buddhapalita and the other exalted teachers:
> To the lineage of the profound teachings on emptiness
>   I bow down.

> And I bow to the glorious Atisha,
> Who in the presence of Buddha was Bhadrapala,
> In Tibet was called Dipamkara Atisha
> And now, in Tushita Heaven, as Nam-kha Tri-ma-me,
> Like a magic jewel works the good of the world.

> And to the feet of the perfect friend and master,
> The Bodhisattva who performed the work of Buddha,
> A precious source fulfilling the two needs:
> To the feet of the spiritual friend Drom I bow.

To Lama Tsongkhapa, crown jewel of Tibetan sages,
Who was an incarnation of the three Bodhisattvas—
Avalokiteshvara, treasure of unapprehendable compassion,
Manjushri, lord of the stainless wisdom,
And Vajrapani, destroyer of Mara's armies:
To Tsongkhapa, Lob-sang Drak-pa, I bow down.

To the lineage Gurus past and present
Who train us in the mystic lore,
Teach us the sutras, tantras, commentaries, and oral traditions
And bestow initiations and blessings, I bow down.

Homage to the Guru, embodiment of the Three Jewels:
The precious Buddha, a peerless teacher,
The precious Dharma, a peerless savior,
And the precious Sangha, a peerless guide.

To Buddha Shakyamuni, Lord of the Shakyas,
Who out of wise compassion was born a prince,
Invincible one who crushed the force of evil:
To he whose body is a golden mountain I bow down.

O lions amongst men,
Buddhas past, present, and future,
To as many of you as exist in the ten directions,
I bow down with body, speech and mind.

On waves of strength of this king
Of praises of exalted, sublime ways,
With bodies numerous as atoms of the world,
I bow down to the Buddhas pervading space.

On every atom is found a Buddha
Sitting amidst countless Bodhisattvas.
In this infinite sphere of mystic beings,
I gaze with eyes of faith.

With oceans of every possible sound
In eulogy of the perfect Buddhas,
I give voice to their excellent qualities:
Hail to those passed to bliss.

2 *Offerings*

Garlands of supreme flowers I offer them;
And beautiful sounds, supreme parasols,
Butter lamps and sacred incense,
I offer to all Awakened Ones.

Excellent food, supreme fragrance,
And a mound of powders as high as Meru
I arrange in mystic formation
And offer to those who have conquered themselves.

All these peerless offerings I hold up
In admiration for those gone to bliss.
In accord with exalted and sublime ways,
I prostrate and make offerings to the Buddhas.

For the practice of confession, which is the third of the seven limbs, it is very important to have the factor of regret; without this factor there is no possibility of purifying the negativities. A proper practice of purification requires four powers—the power of regret, the power of the basis, the actual application of the opponent forces, and the power of resolve. If you have the basic factor of regret, all the other powers will ensue naturally. On the other hand, if you lack the power of regret induced through a proper recognition of negative actions as destructive, then the completion of the other powers is not possible. One's practice of purification will not be effective, since it will not be heartfelt. The great yogi Milarepa said: "When I examined whether or not confession could purify the negativities, I found that it is regret that cleanses them."

In order to generate regret, it is important to see the destructive nature of negative actions and also to understand the law of causality. Causes and effects have a relation between them; in particular, the experiences of suffering and happiness— although having external causes as well—mainly come about due to the state of mind that we have. Based on a disciplined mind, we experience happiness; based on an undisciplined, untamed mind, we undergo suffering. We should think that if we are not able to make any progress from our present state of mind, which always indulges in negative thoughts, there is not much hope for us. So, if we are able to think in such terms, we will be able to really see the destructive nature of negative actions, and also that the store of negative actions that we have is inexhaustible, like a rich person's bank balance. Without the recognition of the destructive nature of the negative forces, we will never be able to develop the deep factor of regret from the depth of our hearts.

If we do not engage in a proper practice of dharma, it seems that we may expend all our store of merit in mundane pleasures. It is very important to have this faculty of regret in our practice of purification and confession.

3 Confession

> Whatever ill deeds I have committed,
> Under the power of desire, anger and ignorance,
> Through my body, speech and mind,
> I confess and purify these individually.

This practice should be followed by the cultivation of admiration and rejoicing in the accumulation of merit by oneself and others.

4 Rejoicing

> In the merits of all sentient beings,
> Solitary realizers, learners and those beyond learning,
> Buddhas in ten directions and their heirs,
> I rejoice in all their virtues.

5   *Requesting to turn the wheel of dharma*

O the light of all universes in ten directions,
Who realized Buddhahood through the stages to
   enlightenment,
I appeal to all of you protectors
To turn the unsurpassed wheel.

6   *Entreating not to enter into Nirvana*

With folded hands I entreat
Those intending to enter nirvana
To live for aeons equal to the atoms on earth,
For the benefit and happiness of all beings.

7   *Dedication*

Whatever little merit I have accumulated,
Through prostrating, offering, confessing,
Rejoicing, requesting and entreating,
I dedicate all towards attaining full enlightenment.

5 The Three Aspirations

Having engaged in the preliminary practices of purifying negativities and accumulating merits within the framework of the
seven limbs, at this point make a fervent prayer to the members of the merit field for the fulfillment of the three aspirations which encompass the essence of that which a practitioner
seeks. The prayer is preceded by the offering of the mandala,
signifying the offering of the entire universe to the objects of
refuge.

MANDALA OFFERING

[Then perform either the long or short versions of the mandala offering:]

> OM VAJRA BHUMI AH HUM, I lay the power-
> ful golden base; OM VAJRA REKHE AH HUM, cir-
> cling outside, the iron fence; in the center, the King
> of Mountains; in the east, the continent Lu-pak-po;
> in the south, Jam-bu-ling; in the west, Ba-lang-jo; in
> the north, Dra-min-yan; off the east continent are the
> islands Lu and Lu-pak; off the south are Nga-yab and
> Nga-yab-zhan; off the west are Yon-dan and Lam-chog-

dro; off the north are Dra-min-yan and Dra-min-yan-kyi-da.

(Above this I place) the jewel mountain, the wish-yielding tree, the magical cow, the untouched harvest, the precious wheel, the precious jewel, the precious queen, the precious minister, the precious elephant, the precious horse, the precious general, the vase filled with a great treasure, and the goddesses of beauty, garlands, song, dance, flowers, incense, light, and perfume. And I place the sun, the moon, a jeweled umbrella, the banner symbolizing total victory, and at the center the best things of men and gods.

All this I hold up and offer to all the holy teachers—my kind root guru and all the gurus of the lineage—and also to Lama Tsongkhapa, who is both Buddha Shakyamuni and Buddha Vajradhara, as well as to the myriads of deities and retinues. For the sake of living beings accept it with compassion and, having enjoyed it, bestow your transforming powers.

Earth blessed with flowers, incense, and scented water
And adorned with the King of Mountains, the four
    continents, and the sun and moon,
I offer to this field of Awakened Beings.
May all beings enjoy this pure sphere.

The body, speech, and mind of both myself and others,
Our possessions, and masses of goodness of the past,
    present, and future,
And the precious mandala of the King of Mountains
    and so forth,
Together with Samantabhadra's peerless offerings,
I mentally claim and offer as a mandala to the lamas,
Yidams, and the Three Precious Jewels;
Out of compassion please accept them
And bestow upon me your transforming powers.
IDAM GURU RATNA MANDALAKAM NIRYATA
    YAMI

Generally speaking, in a practice of offering related to a tantric practice such as *Lama Choepa*, there are different types of offering: outer offerings, associated with the vase initiation; inner offerings, associated with the secret initiation; secret offerings, associated with the wisdom-knowledge initiation; and suchness offerings, associated with the word initiation. The same is true of the mandala offering—there are outer, inner, secret, and suchness mandala offerings.

The internal mandala is the offering of your own physical body, visualizing specific parts of the body as specific parts of the universe.

Perceiving all of them as manifestations of the union of bliss and emptiness, and also seeing them as the mere sport and manifestation of the subtle wind (energy) and mind is the suchness mandala offering.

When you make the outer mandala offering, you can do the visualizations of the universe as described in the mandala formula. But that does not mean that you have to accept that the universe exists in such a manner, with Mount Meru, the four continents, and so forth. It is always important when studying a text to take into account the time, the community, and the mentality of the people when the particular text was written or taught. Ancient Buddhist treatises describe the universe in conformity with the popular theory of the universe current at that time. Consequently, the descriptions differ from those found in modern cosmology.

The point is to offer the entire universe—your own possessions and also things that do not belong to you. Doing this signifies the overcoming of even a subtle form of possessiveness and attachment, but does not mean that we have to accept that the universe system exists as explained in the Abhidharma texts. After all, the basic approach of the Buddhist is to subject concepts to rigorous logical processes, and if anything contradicts direct observation and logic, it should not be accepted just because it is taught in the sutras or the texts. The earth of scientific experimentation and observation—its size and relative position in the solar system—is the earth that we live in, and its appearance is common to the beings living in this world. I think that the scientific observations on this matter are beyond dispute and have to be taken as the truth; otherwise, there is a danger of causing misunderstanding in others who, because of not understanding the profound philosophy of Buddhism, might despise it for certain of its views on cosmology.

PRAYER OF THE THREE ASPIRATIONS

Next, make a prayer that may you, not only in this lifetime but also always in future lifetimes, never be separated from the kind care of a spiritual master. Also, request—with the three great aspirations, as one finds in *Lamrim Chenmo*—the spiritual masters to help free you from all the obstacles that hinder you from achieving high realizations. The three great aspirations are:

> May all deluded views, ranging from not being respect-
> ful to the gurus to the subtle forms of duality, cease;
> May all the positive states of mind, ranging from be-
> ing respectful to the gurus to the final achievement
> of union, be realized within; and
> May all external and internal obstacles to the realiza-
> tion of these two aspirations be overcome.

These aspirations include and encompass all the aspirations of a spiritual practitioner: to be free of all the obstacles and to obtain all the factors necessary for the realizations. There is nothing more that a practitioner could seek.

6 *Invoking the Inspiring Power of the Lineage*

PRAYERS TO THE LINEAGE MASTERS

O precious, holy Root Guru,
Sit upon a lotus and moon on my head;
Hold me within your great compassion
And bestow siddhis of body, speech, and mind.

O peerless teacher, transcended Buddha,
O holy regent, invincible Maitreya,
And Asanga, who was prophesied by Buddha,
To Buddha and these two bodhisattvas I pray.

O Vasubhandu, crown jewel of Indian sages,
And Vimuktisena, who achieved the Middle View,
And Vimuktisenagomin, in whom I place faith:
To these three, who have opened the world's eyes, I
    pray.

O Paramasena, wondrous and splendid one,
O Vinitasena, master of the profound path,
And Vairochana, treasury of vast deeds:
To these three friends of the living I pray.

O Haribhadra, propagator of the profound wisdom-
teachings,
O Kusali, holder of oral traditions,
And Ratnasena, savior of the living beings:
To these three spiritual guides I pray.

O Serlingpa, who found the heart of bodhi,
O Atisha, upholder of this great vehicle,
And Drom Rinpoche, elucidator of the good path:
To these three pillars of the doctrine I pray.

O peerless teacher Shakyamuni,
O Manjushri, embodiment of all Buddha's knowledge,
And Nagarjuna, seer of the profoundest meaning:
To these three crown ornaments of teachers I pray.

O Chandrakirti, clarifier of Nagarjuna's thought,
O Vidyakokila, the great disciple of Chandrakirti,
And Vidyakokila the Second, a second son:
To these three lords of the lineage I pray.

O Atisha, upholder of this great vehicle,
Who sees the profundity of dependent arising,
And O Drom Rinpoche, elucidator of this good path:
To these two ornaments of the world I bow.

O Gon-pa-wa, lord of mystics,
O Neu-zu-pa, whose support is deep samadhi,
And Tak-ma-pa, upholder of the teachings on dis-
cipline:
To these three lights amongst the barbarians I pray.

O Nam-seng, whose practice is spontaneous,
O Nam-kha Gyal-po, he blessed by the holy,
And Sang-gye-zang, he free of worldly passions:
To these sublime sons of Buddha I pray.

O Nam-kha Gyal-tsen, who is blessed
And guarded by the meditational deities
And who is a supreme spiritual friend
To the beings of this dark age: to you I pray.

O Po-to-wa, image of Buddha himself,
O Sha-ra-wa, whose intellect is beyond challenge,
And Che-kha-wa, teacher of the bodhimind:
To these three fulfillers of hope I pray.

O Chil-pu-pa, lord of scriptures and insight,
O Lha-lung Wang-chuk, a supreme sage,
And Gon-po Rinpoche, savior of the three worlds:
To these great ones I pray.

O Zang-chen-pa, who radiates with control,
O Tso-na-wa, lord of the scriptures on discipline,
And Mon-dra-pa, master of Abhidharma:
To these three navigators of the world I pray.

O Dhol-yob Zang-po, glorious lama
Who has found the vast and profound dharma
Who upholds the doctrine through enlightened action,
And protects the fortunate: to you I pray.

O Trul-trim Bar, lord of the siddhas,
O Shon-nu Od, who relied well on many masters,
And Gyer Gon-pa, whose mind is one with the
    Mahayana:
To these three sons of Buddha I pray.

O Sang-gye Won, treasury of marvelous qualities,
O Nam-kha Gyal-po, he blessed by the holy,
And Sang-gye-zang, he free of worldly passions:
To these three gentle bodhisattvas I pray.

O Nam-kha Gyal-tsen, who is blessed
And guarded by the meditational deities
And who is a supreme spiritual friend
To the beings of this dark age: to you I pray.

And to Tsongkhapa, crown jewel of Tibetan sages,
Who was an incarnation of the three bodhisattvas—
Avalokiteshvara, the treasure of unapprehendable com-
    passion,
Manjushri, lord of the stainless wisdom,
And Vajrapani, destroyer of Mara's armies:
To Tsongkhapa, Lob-zang Drak-pa, I pray.

And O Jam-pal Gya-tso, lord of siddhis,
O Khe-drub Ge-lek Pal, a son amongst adepts and
    teachers,
And Ba-so Je, a mine of ear-whispered lineages:
To these three peerless lamas I pray.

O Cho-kyi Dor-je, he attained to great union,
O Gyal-wa En-sa-pa, he who is three Buddha-kayas,
And Sang-gye Ye-she, lord of scriptures and insight:
To these three sagely adepts I pray.

O eyes through whom the vast scriptures are seen,
Supreme doors for the fortunate who would cross over
    to spiritual freedom,
Illuminators whose wise means vibrate with com-
    passion:
To the entire line of mystic friends I pray.

While reciting prayers to the lineage gurus of the Lamrim
practice, visualize nectar descending from the individual
figures, and imagine that you receive the inspiration of the particular masters which purifies any negativities committed in
relation to them, thus enhancing your mind's receptivity to
the realization of the path. You should then visualize a dupli-

cate of your spiritual master descending to your crown; request the buddhas and bodhisattvas to shower their blessings and inspiration on you because, induced by a genuine desire to practice Lamrim from within, you are now embarking upon a proper spiritual path.

When you recite the verses making requests to these figures, repeat the last line of each verse. During the first recitation, visualize nectars flowing from the particular masters of the lineage, and during the second, visualize a replica of the individual figures dissolving into you.

Then imagine that your mind is made receptive to the realization of the specific practices of the Lamrim—for example, proper reliance on a spiritual master, and the recognition of the importance of human birth. Think that you and all other sentient beings have actually achieved the realizations. At this point you could also perform the visualization of the protectors expelling obstacles and providing you with favorable conditions for your practice.

7 *Reviewing the Stages of the Path*

Following a kind master, foundation of all perfections,
Is the very root and basis of the path.
Empower me to see this clearly
And to make every effort to follow him well.

Precious human life gained but once
Has great potential but is easily lost.
Empower me to remember this constantly
And to think day and night of taking its essence.

I must remember that death is quick to strike,
For spirit quivers in flesh like a bubble in water;
And after death one's good and evil deeds
Trail after one like the shadow trails the body.

Understanding that this most certainly is true,
May I discard every level of wrong
And generate an infinite mass of goodness;
Empower me to be thus continually aware.

Sensual gluttony is a gate to suffering
And is not worthy of a lucid mind.

Empower me to realize the shortcomings of samsara
And to give birth to the great wish for blissful freedom.

And empower me that with mindfulness and alertness
Born from thoughts ultimately pure,
I may live in accord with the holy dharma,
The ways leading to personal liberation.

Just as I myself have fallen into samsara's waters
So have all other sentient beings.
Empower me to see this and really to practice
Bodhimind, that carries the weight of freeing them.

Yet without habituation to the three spiritual disciplines,
Thought-training accomplishes no enlightenment.
Empower me to know this deeply, and intensely to train
In the various ways of the great bodhisattvas.

And empower me to pacify distorted mental wanderings
And to decipher the ultimate meaning in life,
That I may give birth within my mindstream
To the path combining concentration and vision.

He who trains in these common Mahayana practices
Becomes a vessel worthy of the Supreme Vehicle, Vajrayana.
Empower me that I may quickly and easily
Arrive at that portal of fortunate beings.

The foundation of what then produces the two powers
Is the guarding of the pledges and commitments of
tantric initiation.
Bless me so that I may have uncontrived knowledge
of this
And guard my disciplines as I do my very life.

Bless me so that I may gain realization of the main practices
Of the two stages of Vajrayana, essence of the tantric path;
And, by sitting relentlessly in four daily sessions of yoga,
Actualize just what the sages have taught.

Empower me that the masters who have unfolded the sublime path within me
And the spiritual friends who have inspired me may live long;
And that the myriads of inner and outer interferences
Be completely and utterly calmed forever.

In all future lives may I never be parted
From the perfect lamas or the pure ways of dharma.
May I gain every experience of the paths and stages
And quickly attain the stage of Holder of Diamond Knowledge.

While reciting the above verses entitled *Yonten Shigyurma* (Foundation of All Perfections) mentally review all the stages of the spiritual path. At the end, make fervent aspirations that, should death seize you before you have achieved high realizations, you may be reborn as a human endowed with leisure and fortune so that you can continue the journey along the Lamrim path leading to complete enlightenment in future lives. Thus dedicate your merit to the fulfillment of this aim and that of being able to work for the benefit of all beings.

8 Dissolution of the Merit Field

Having beseeched the merit field for fulfillment of the three aspirations, you should start the process of the dissolution of the merit field, as the preparatory practices are now coming to their end.

The process begins with an exclusive request to your root spiritual guru made in conjunction with the recitation of the following verse:

> O, my glorious and precious root guru,
> Reside at my crown on a lotus seat,
> And sustain me with great kindness,
> By bestowing the attainments of your body, speech and
>   mind.

If you have visualized the elaborate version of the merit field, now imagine that light rays emanate from the heart of Shakyamuni Buddha and touch all the members of the merit field surrounding him. They melt into light and gradually dissolve into the lineage masters of the Vast Practice and the Profound View, which in turn dissolve respectively into Maitreya and Manjushri. Similarly, the masters of the Experiential Lineage dissolve into Vajradhara, and the host of gurus from whom you have received teachings in person dissolve into your personal root guru. At this point you should reaffirm your visualization of the five figures. After a while, visualize Maitreya and Manjushri dissolving into the central figure while their thrones and cushions dissolve into those of Buddha Shakyamuni. Eventually, your own root guru melts into light and dissolves into Buddha Shakyamuni's heart. Vajradhara, progressively diminishing in size, enters through Buddha Shakyamuni's crown and remains within his heart as a wisdom being. Cultivate a clear visualization at this point of Buddha Shakyamuni, who eventually dissolves into your personal root guru seated at your crown. Your root guru is in the aspect of Buddha Shakyamuni, possessing all the qualities of a completely enlightened being.

Then, focusing upon your root guru at your crown, make a single-pointed request from the depths of your heart. Together with all the sentient beings around you, make request prayers to the spiritual master, seeing him from the depths of your heart as the embodiment of all the objects of refuge. Perceive the spiritual master as the embodiment of the dharmakaya, all the bodies of the Buddha, meditational deities, heroes, heroines, and so forth. Do this until you feel some effect within your mind; at that point it is effective to examine the nature of the mind which feels that experience.

Say to the master that he alone is the embodiment of all refuges and that you entrust yourself completely to his care and request his inspiration.

SINGLE-POINTED PRAYER

> I beseech you, Buddha Vajradhara,
> The exalted guru deity embodying the four kayas.
> I beseech you, Buddha Vajradhara,
> The exalted guru deity embodying the unobscured
>   dharmakaya.
> I beseech you, Buddha Vajradhara,
> The exalted guru deity of blissful sambhogakaya.
> I beseech you, Buddha Vajradhara,

The exalted guru deity of manifold nirmanakaya.
I beseech you, Buddha Vajradhara,
The exalted guru deity embodying all gurus.
I beseech you, Buddha Vajradhara,
The exalted guru deity embodying all meditational
    deities.
I beseech you, Buddha Vajradhara,
The exalted guru deity embodying all buddhas
I beseech you, Buddha Vajradhara,
The exalted guru deity embodying all sublime dharma.
I beseech you, Buddha Vajradhara,
The exalted guru deity embodying all sangha.
I beseech you, Buddha Vajradhara,
The exalted guru deity embodying all dakinis.
I beseech you, Buddha Vajradhara,
The exalted guru deity embodying all protectors.
I beseech you, Buddha Vajradhara,
The exalted guru deity embodying all refuges.

While reciting these verses pray fervently and imagine that, because the guru is pleased with you, nectar descends from his body and enters through your crown. This purifies all the negativities that you have committed in connection with him, and the inspiration you receive empowers you to achieve all the high realizations on the path. With that, the practices preliminary to the practice of proper reliance on a spiritual master are over.

Just as in a sadhana of tantric meditation there is a point where one does the meditations on subtle and coarse generation stage practices, similarly it is at this point that one undertakes the actual practices of Lamrim meditation.

9 *Activities of the Between-Session Periods*

At the end of the session, take a little rest. Sometimes when you are resting, you may have inspiration all of a sudden, which helps you see things that you have never seen before.

Although in the after-session periods you are not engaged in formal meditation, you should keep your mind deep down still focused on the practice so that the warmth of the session is not lost. Then, when you resume your second session you will be able to conduct it successfully, thus enabling you to build on the progress you have made in the first session. Otherwise, if you let yourself stray and be idle during the between-session periods, whatever progress you may have made in the first session will be totally lost, and then in the second session you will have to start right from the beginning. The state is analogous to a hearth in which you do not extinguish the fire totally, so that when you rekindle the fire you will be able to do so quite easily and quickly. It is also helpful to read texts related to your practice.

When you wake up in the morning, you should bless your speech with certain mantras and develop a strong determination that you will use the twenty-four hours of the day for a worthy purpose and shall not waste even a single moment of the day. With such determination and motivation at the beginning, do any practices that you undertake, such as guru yoga, and then engage in the practice of Lamrim.

If you live your life in such a manner you will be able to make progress, whereas if you just give up right from the beginning and feel discouraged, then there is not much you can hope for. Therefore, it is very important to have courage and determination. The same is true for lay people: Although you have to be concerned about your profession, livelihood, and so forth, nevertheless, at the beginning of the day when you first wake up, it is important to develop the firm determination that you shall live the day properly, in a righteous manner, and not deceive others, tell lies, and so forth. Tibetans, for example, should make the determination that during the day, if they are not able to make any contribution to the Tibetan cause, at least they will not degrade the Tibetan name or be a disgrace to it. Those Tibetans who hold me dear should determine that at least they will think about the Dalai Lama, and not be deceptive to him.

Therefore, monks, lay people, and all of you, it is possible to live a life properly within the dharma, right from the beginning of the day adopting the right attitude and determination, putting all that you know about dharma into practice, with a plan that the things you are not able to practice right now, you will practice next year or in the future. In such a manner you will be able to make progress.

At the end of the day when you go to bed, before going to sleep you should check on the nature of the activities in which you engaged during the day. If you find that any negative actions have been performed, you should generate regret and resolve that you will never indulge in them in the future. If you find that you have engaged in some positive actions, you should rejoice.

Also, when going to bed, it is important that you do so with a virtuous thought, because sometimes it is possible for a practitioner to have certain practices in dreams, too; this will be particularly important for the morning, when you are waking up, because in the morning you have a very clear, fresh mind and therefore, when you engage in a practice at that time, it will be more powerful and clear.

Those meditators who are up in caves should be careful not to meet just anybody, because such a meeting may hinder their progress. Even the mere indication of a stranger coming may hinder your practices; therefore, be cautious.

This is how you should meditate and undertake the practice of dharma. If you are able to undertake the practice in such a manner, irrespective of whether you recite many texts or not, you will be able to make real progress. Then there is a hope that you will be able to achieve enlightenment in this lifetime, or, if not, in the intermediate state, or in a future lifetime.

10 Summary

All the stages of the preliminary practices as explained in the last two chapters within the framework of what are called the six preparatory practices are common to all the topics of Lamrim meditation and therefore precede every meditative session. These stages prepare not only the physical environment where the meditation is undertaken but most importantly the practitioner's mind, making it receptive to the spiritual change that he or she is likely to go through in the meditative process. As you can notice, the preliminary practices discussed here are based on the standard preliminary rite text *Jorchoe* (Six Preparatory Practices), and the visualizations involved are explained rather extensively. However, as you progress along the path of meditation, and depending upon the length of time you have, you could spend less time with the preliminary practices. Such a shorter session could be undertaken based on just a single verse on each of the important elements of the practice, for example, seven limbs, refuge, generation of the altruistic motive, mandala offering, request to the lineage masters, dedication, etc.

Having prepared yourself through such a preliminary process you should then engage in the main meditation. In the case of every meditation topic of Lamrim—for example, the proper reliance on a spiritual teacher—the actual meditation is done right after the dissolution of the merit field. At that point all the members of the merit field are already dissolved into the principal figure of the merit field, which is your own root guru in the form of Buddha Shakyamuni. Your root guru also goes through a progressive diminution in size, eventually becoming the size of a thumb. He then descends to your crown where he is visualized as being seated facing the same direction as you are. While focusing single-pointedly on your guru at your crown, make fervent requests to him. Meditatively imagine that, by the force of your prayer request, nectars and light rays flow from your guru's body, fill your entire body and cleanse the physical and mental stains that obtruct you from attaining the realization of a proper reliance on a spiritual teacher. Imagine that your mind is made receptive to such an experience. You can now begin your meditation on the actual chosen topic.

In conclusion, again visualize that light rays and nectars descend from the guru's body and fill your body, thus infusing your entire being with his inspiring power. Your meditative seesion should then be ended with a dedication of all the positive energy that you have accumulated from this particular session towards the happiness of all living beings. The between-session practices recommended in the case of guru devotion meditation are appropriate for all the subsequent meditations as well.

PART III:
MAIN LAMRIM MEDITATIONS

1 Reliance on a Spiritual Teacher

You should think now that the reason that you and all other sentient beings revolve in the cycle of existence and undergo all these undesirable sufferings and so forth, is that you and they lack realization of the proper relation to a spiritual master. Therefore, request the spiritual masters to give the inspiration to make you overcome obstacles that hinder you from realizing this path.

The actual practice of proper reliance on a spiritual teacher is divided into two: reliance through thought and reliance through action.

RELIANCE THROUGH THOUGHT

Cultivating Faith and Conviction
First, you should visualize your spiritual master at your crown. The spiritual master is the embodiment of all the buddhas. From his heart light rays emanate and in front of him are all the gurus from whom you have received teachings directly.

Visualize all of them in their normal appearance, with all their physical and personality defects, if they have any. To visualize them with all their seeming faults and defects is important at this point, since you are now engaged in a specific meditation on guru devotion which involves—to a great extent—the means to overcome your perception of faults in them.

Then, reflect upon the great benefits of proper reliance on a spiritual master—the eight benefits[17] as outlined in the Lam-rim, such as getting closer to the achievement of buddhahood. By referring to authentic scriptural sources, by employing all sorts of reasonings most suitable to your mind, by considering examples from the lives of the past masters—that is, by employing any means at your disposal—you should be able to see the great benefits of relying on a spiritual master. It is a very profitable venture!

Therefore, develop the conviction that you should properly rely on him or her. Rejoice in the fact that you have such an opportunity. You should not have the notion that "spiritual master" only refers to high lamas who give teachings from high thrones; rather, the reference is to the spiritual master to whom you relate daily, who leads you on the spiritual path step by step. The kindness of such a guru is the greatest.

Your faith should be reasoned faith, not just blind faith, based on proper intelligence so that when people question and attempt to refute your belief and practice, you will be able to withstand their arguments. Therefore, your faith should be properly based on a firm foundation. If you have this faculty of intelligence, you will be invulnerable to arguments. Otherwise, as the Kadampa masters say, "Faith alone is like a blind person, and it can be led anywhere by anyone if it lacks the complementary factor of wisdom." So the faith that is supported by the factor of wisdom, and likewise the compassion that is supported by wisdom, is indispensable in a Buddhist practice, whereas faith and compassion alone are common features of all major religions. Therefore, if you cultivate a faith based on a proper foundation, it will be rational and therefore very stable.

The second step is to think about the disadvantages of not relating to a spiritual master and then, weighing the disadvantages and advantages of relating and not relating to a master, decide that you shall relate to a master. As Lama Tsongkhapa advised in *Lamrim Chenmo*, first it is important to apply all sorts of contemplations; as a conclusion you should develop a deep conviction and make the determination that you must now definitely rely on a spiritual teacher.

Furthermore, seeing that through such a reliance you stand to gain, and that without it you stand to lose, pray that you may have an opportunity for such a reliance in all future lives as well. Think: I wish never to lack the guidance of a qualified master in my future lives; therefore, I decide today to rely on a spiritual master right here and now. That is the decision you have to make.

Reflect now, as a third step, upon the disadvantages and harm of having a breach in your guru devotion practice.[18] You will have all sorts of adverse circumstances within this lifetime, and the damage they will cause for your future lives will be great. Therefore, after seeing the harm and disadvantages of having such a breach, you should decide that you will never permit it to occur. Regarding this, it might be helpful to reflect upon stories of the great masters, such as those describing how Naropa in India related to his master Tilopa and how Milarepa in Tibet underwent hardships in fulfilling the wishes of his spiritual teachers and never had any breach in his practice. Having decided that you will rely on a spiritual master, you should determine never to make a breach in your relationship.

The actual process of relying on the guru through thought includes, first, cultivating faith in the spiritual master. For this, while focusing on the spiritual masters in front of you, think that the reason that all the spiritual masters appear to you as though they were ordinary beings is that you have an inferior state of mind and are not able to see them in their own nature as true buddhas.

There are scriptural sources in which Buddha Vajradhara himself says that in future times he will take the form of spiritual masters. Think that it is because of his great kindness that Buddha Vajradhara has assumed the forms of ordinary beings as spiritual masters, in order to suit the practitioners like yourself who have no faculty to see the buddhas directly in their natural aspect.

A Tibetan master said: "If you understand, not just in mere words, the way in which buddhas and bodhisattvas of the past help the beings of the present age, you will see it comes down to the qualified gurus." Therefore, the kindest spiritual master is the one who gives you teachings, because he is the one who leads you to the achievement of enlightenment. If the buddhas are working for the benefit of us at all, it is only through the gurus. So, if you think along such lines, you will be able to generate deep faith in the spiritual master.

Approaching the topic from a different angle, you should reflect that although the spiritual masters are, in fact, true buddhas, their not appearing to us as such is due to our own ignorance. At this point, it is helpful to reflect that Asanga saw his master Maitreya in the form of a dog, and that Maitripa saw his guru Savaripa as an ordinary hunter, and that Legpa Karma saw the Buddha as having all sorts of faults. Think that it is because of your ignorant mind that you are not able to see spiritual masters as true buddhas. Perceptions in general are deceptive. You can conclude that since your own perception is unreliable, you will never generate even a single thought of perceiving fault in the master.

Reflect that there must be manifestations of the Buddha who are actively working for your benefit; if there are such beings, they are probably your spiritual masters. But then the thought might arise that you see all sorts of faults in them. Analyze whether this perception is illusory or not: if they are true buddhas, how can they have faults? It is only your own perception that is unreliable.

As the Panchen Lama says here, the appearance of these faults is not because your spiritual masters have faults, but rather because they are using skillful means by portraying such faults in order to show themselves as ordinary beings so that you can relate to them more easily.

How can we ordinary beings, whose minds are always under the influence of ignorance, determine what is true and what is false with great certainty? Our judgments, even concerning ordinary things, are frequently clouded by our emotions. For example, we often see the actions of our loved ones—even if they are harmful—as wonderful, whereas we judge even the positive actions of a person we dislike as pretentious and false. We cannot rely upon our own perceptions; it is a fact that we misapprehend many situations. If this is a general fact, how can we still stubbornly maintain that our perceptions about our own spiritual masters must be true?

Sometimes it is effective to take as the central figure of the merit field the spiritual master to whom you feel most distant and in whom you feel you see faults. You can also visualize this master, in whom you find it most difficult to develop faith, as the wisdom being at the heart of Buddha Shakyamuni. Then reflect upon his qualities—his body, personality, and so forth. This practice will actually help you to overcome perceptions of faults in all spiritual masters. It is very difficult to perceive all spiritual masters as true buddhas, but it is possible to overcome perceptions of faults. If you were to suspend your practices until you could see all the masters as buddhas, it would be a long wait until you could commence your practices. Overcoming the perception of faults lays a good foundation within your mind for other practices such as refuge, renunciation, and so forth, and the progress you make in these practices will increase your faith in spiritual masters. So, the point that is most indispensable at the initial stage is the overcoming of misconceptions about faults in the spiritual master.

Without your masters' proper guidance, how can you have the knowledge of the paths, let alone embark upon the right one? That you have the knowledge to embark upon a spiritual path and to discriminate between right and wrong is due to the Buddha's kindness in appearing in an ordinary form to teach you. Therefore, you all should reflect that the little understanding that you have about the stages of the path, and the little practice that you can do with the hope of planting some seed in your minds, is due to the kindness of the spiritual master. Without the guidance of the gurus you might be able to read some texts, but integrating the teachings with your own minds through proper instruction is possible only by following the advice of a teacher. It is only through his kindness that you will be able to accomplish such a feat.

By thinking in such terms, you will find that the kindness of a spiritual master is great, and greater still is his appearing in the present form so that you can have direct access to him. For example, if a person who has very high rank comes with his guards displaying all the grandeur of his position to help someone who is very sick and bereaved, it may not be very helpful; on the other hand, if he comes as an ordinary person, without any servants and so forth, he can be more helpful to the troubled person and may deeply touch the patient's mind. Similarly, the appearance of the buddhas in their *sambhogakaya* (enjoyment body) form may not be as beneficial to you as their appearance in the form of spiritual masters. The buddhas in their sambhogakaya form are accessible only to bodhisattvas on high levels.

So you should realize that through the great kindness of the spiritual master, at this time of degeneration still the buddhas are able to portray themselves to you in a physical form and help you according to your own disposition. It is almost like they are protecting those who are abandoned by all other refuges. When you think in such terms, you will really begin to appreciate the great kindness of the spiritual masters, which surpasses the kindness of all others. Such forms of reflection will enable you to actually see the perception of faults in the guru as helpful for increasing faith in his skillful means. Thinking in such terms will increase faith and respect in the guru. So that is how you cultivate faith and conviction in the spiritual master.

Without faith, even though you might have a very clear visualization and image of the spiritual master, it will not be very effective—it is almost like having a clear image of a good painting. So, develop single-pointed faith and respect for the spiritual master. Such a faith in the guru, firmly based on the realization of him as a true Buddha, can come about only when you have first developed a general understanding of the entire framework of the Buddhist path. For a person who possesses such knowledge, the recitation of even a short guru yoga text can become a profound guru devotion practice. It is for this reason that I always emphasize the importance of study for Buddhist practitioners. It is very difficult to explain the importance of guru devotion to someone not familiar with Buddhist doctrines because if such a person is doubtful of the possibility of buddhahood in the first place, there is not much point in repeating that Vajradhara has said that the spiritual masters are manifestations of the buddhas.

Therefore, first of all it is very important to have some understanding of emptiness and the law of interdependence and how they are complementary. This will enable you to develop deep conviction in the law of causality, which in turn will enable you to develop conviction in things that are beyond the perception of ordinary beings, thus helping you to have conviction in the Three Jewels.

You can reason that if the spiritual master Buddha Shakyamuni has proved truthful and reliable on very profound matters—like emptiness and impermanence—then his statement that the spiritual master is the manifestation of the Buddha can also be relied upon. Approaching the topic in such a manner will enable you to develop a deep faith and conviction in the Buddha's doctrine; following the stages of the path found in Lamrim will then be very fruitful. Without such a basis, the practice of guru devotion may not be so beneficial and appealing at the beginning.

Cultivating Respect

It is through recollecting the great kindness of the spiritual master that one cultivates respect. Now, again focusing upon the master that you have visualized in front of you, reflect that the understanding you develop of the entire path is due to his kindness. Because of the force of this contemplation, nectar descends and so forth.

The guru's kindness includes the kindness of giving you teachings and taming your mind and so forth. You should mentally review the great kindness of the individual spiritual masters, beginning with those who taught you the alphabet and how to read, and including those who gave teachings on the treatises; monastic, bodhisattva, and tantric vows; commentaries on generation and completion stages of tantra; transmissions and so forth; and even advice as to the way you lead your life. So the entire way of life and outlook are taught by the spiritual masters.

When you think in such terms, you will truly be able to see the great kindness of the spiritual master; his kindness surpasses that of Buddha Shakyamuni. From the point of view of qualifications, all the buddhas are equal, but from the point of view of kindness, the spiritual master's kindness far exceeds that of the buddhas.

Having perceived the master as the Buddha, cultivate strong faith, and, reflecting upon his kindness, develop deep respect for him. That is how to relate to a spiritual master through thought.

RELIANCE THROUGH ACTION

This practice is done by following the teachings that the spiritual master has given, living according to his advice, and making offerings to him and serving him.

Although living according to his advice is the real offering to a master, if you find that any part of the master's advice contradicts the general mode of approach of the Buddhist doctrine, you should examine it and then explain to the spiritual master why you cannot fulfill that advice. As Ashvagosha said in his *Guru Panchashika* (Fifty Verses on the Guru), "Regarding the directions that are unfit, explain their unsuitability in words." Also, Gunaprabha in his *Vinayasutra* (The Condensed Essence of Ethics) said, "Reverse the directions if they are unwholesome." In the same vein, a Mahayana sutra reads, "Comply well with the advice that accords with the positive ideals, and act contrary to that which is against the principles.'' There are some exceptions where the spiritual master sees very special benefits for a certain individual; then, although the advice may not directly accord with the general approach of Buddhist doctrine, it is nevertheless given. I am telling you all this from my own experience; not everything I say should be accepted by you. If what the Dalai Lama says accords with the general mode of approach of the Buddha's doctrine and seems sensible, then you should follow it; if you find that anything that the Dalai Lama says contradicts the general approach of the Buddha's doctrine, you should just leave it. This is an important point.

If you do not apply this caution, there is a danger that a person who claims to be a spiritual master but who is ignorant of the Buddha's doctrine may give some advice that could prove harmful. Then, both the disciples and the master will harm themselves.

Therefore, it is very important to judge whether or not the direction given accords with the framework of the Buddhist doctrine encompassed in the *Tripitaka* (Three Scriptural Collections).[19] Many people in the West mistakenly term Tibetan Buddhism *Lamaism*;[20] so, there is also a danger, if you are not very careful, of really making it Lamaism in the true sense of that word. This point has been greatly emphasized by Lama Tsongkhapa in his *Lamrim Chenmo*.

CONCLUDING ACTIVITIES

While meditating on the practice of reliance, make requests to the spiritual masters in front of you. In a *sadhana*, when one feels exhausted by the meditation, at the end one can do the repetition of mantras; in the same manner here, after you do the specific meditations on Lamrim, you should follow with the rest of the recitation and repetition of the guru's name mantra or praise verses. Invoke your master's inspiration, and dedicate all the merit that you have gained through such a practice to the benefit of all beings. You can again visualize nectar descending from the spiritual master at your crown, and passing down through your body, or you could do the visualization of the guru himself descending through your crown and entering into your heart, remaining there inseparably. This is a very powerful practice, which will make you invulnerable to negative actions, because you will always feel that the guru is there to witness all your actions.

Although the practice of proper reliance on a spiritual master is contemplative in nature, at the end of the contemplation you should do absorptive meditations as well, dwelling on the conclusion. This combined practice of contemplation and absorption is necessary.

You should end each session of Lamrim practice before you become exhausted; otherwise, if you try to make sessions very long, you may feel so tired that you will not want to repeat them. Therefore, initially it is very important to end the session when you are not yet tired, so that your practice of dharma will be steady like a stream, not momentary like water gushing out of a broken tank, emptying the tank in a few minutes.

2 Recognizing the Human Potential

The first of the practices based on a proper reliance on a spiritual master is the persuading of oneself to take the essence of having obtained a human life of leisure and opportunity.

First it is important to recognize the human form as rare and precious. It is not enough just to obtain this precious human form which has great potential; rather, you should use that potential to its fullest extent by taking its essence. For example, if a person's ascent to high office is not followed by good work for the community and people, it is not very beneficial and worthwhile. If, on the basis of full use of the potential, one is able to accomplish great feats, that would truly be a great success. Therefore, it is important initially to recognize all the significance and great potential of this human existence.

What is the meaning of human existence endowed with leisure[21] and fortune? *Leisure* refers to having time, just as the word is ordinarily used when one asks whether or not people have the time to do such and such. Therefore, this term refers to a human existence that has the time to undertake the practice.

Other forms of existence, such as animals, do not have the chance to think about dharma because they are under the strong influence of ignorance. Compared to them, we human beings are amply endowed with the leisure and capacity to practice dharma.

So, just as the masters said, if you were to take rebirth right now in the lower realms, then the doctrine of the buddhas and the teachings of tantra, although they might exist in this world, would not be of much benefit to you. Although you might take favorable forms of existence in *deva* realms and so forth, since the practice of dharma has to be undertaken on the basis of enhancing one's mind, and since in such realms one's mind is under strong influences, you would not have the opportunity that you have right now. But this is not the case with you.

Furthermore, you have not taken rebirth at a time when the Buddha's doctrine has totally lived out its duration of benefit. Rather, it is still active and very much relevant. But even though you have taken rebirth at such a time, if you were born in a country where dharma was totally inaccessible, then you would not benefit from your human existence. This is not the case with you either.

Even though you have taken rebirth in a country or community where dharma is available, if you were to lack physical and mental capabilities, you would not be able to benefit from its availability. This is not the case, nor is it the case that you are under the influence of wrong views, such as the total negation of the possibility of rebirth or the authenticity of dharma. Whether or not you have cultivated a deep conviction derived from valid cognition, you do have a certain understanding of dharma that is powerful enough to persuade you to take an interest in it.

Therefore, at this juncture, if you probe you will find that you are free of most of the obvious adverse conditions for the practice of dharma and that you are equipped with favorable conditions. You are free from lack of leisure, and on top of that you possess what are called the ten endowments,[22] personal and circumstantial. You have been born at a time when, although the Buddha is not still alive, his doctrine is still alive and you can meet a living spiritual master. Also, you can emulate certain exemplary personalities who have gained high realizations by engaging in such a practice. So, if you think in such terms, you will be really able to admire and rejoice in the present opportunity.

After you reflect along these lines, it is very important that you finally make a conclusion and decide on the basis of this human existence to explore its potential to its fullest extent by engaging in a serious practice of dharma. So, request the spiritual master at your crown to grant you the inspiration to overcome the obstacles to your realizations. On the basis of this precious human form, you will be able to accomplish great feats—not only the assurance of well-being in future lifetimes, but also the fulfillment of the final aspiration.

Chandrakirti, in his *Guide to the Middle Way*, chapter two, said:

> If one doesn't restrain oneself (from one's downfalls)
> When one is free and lives agreeably,
> How can one raise oneself in the future,
> When one falls into an abyss and is at others' mercy?

RARITY OF HUMAN EXISTENCE

Having reflected upon the great significance and potential of human existence, you should reflect upon its rarity. Although something might be rare, if it does not have any potential to bring about great benefit, it is not very precious. Present human existence is not like that. Not only is it rare to find, it also has great potential; on its basis one will not only be able to attain a higher rebirth, but can also obtain the omniscient state.

Since the beginning of life on this planet, for more than five billion years, many forms of life have existed and have gone through a process of evolution. Of all these forms, one finds that the human form is the most sophisticated, in terms of having not only a positive capacity but also a destructive one.

Humans possess a very sophisticated brain, which has great power and capability, and are endowed with a faculty that enables them to plan things and judge between right and wrong. So, among all the forms of life, one finds no history that can compare with that of human beings.

Besides the category of phenomena that are obvious to one, phenomena that are hidden to one at present, such as the momentary nature of things, the emptiness of inherent existence, and so forth, can also eventually be understood on the basis of a human body employing the human faculties. Furthermore, on this basis one will be able to cultivate the very strong force of the altruistic attitude as well as receive very profound vows—tantric, bodhicitta, or monastic—with which one will be able to accumulate great stores of merit. Therefore, from all these points of view—those of ultimate and temporary aims—the human body is equipped with a great capacity.

You should rejoice that you have obtained such a body and should decide never to waste its potential. If the effort is made on your part, you will be able to attain great achievements. Many masters of the past, Indian and Tibetan masters of all the great traditions, achieved their high realizations on the basis of the human form. Regarded as a basis, the human body that you possess, and the bodies of the great beings, have no difference between them. Think that, like the great masters who achieved high realizations on the basis of this precious human body and achieved the completely enlightened state, you also will work for the achievement of the omniscient state on the basis of this present human existence. You have obtained this great opportunity; if you do not take the initiative right now, when will you? It is now or never. That is how you should reflect.

By emulating the examples of great personalities of the past, by pondering upon scriptural quotations and anecdotes taught by teachers, by employing all sorts of means, you should be able to develop a deep conviction that this present human body has great potential and that you shall never waste even a single minute of its use. On the other hand, not taking any essence of this precious human existence, but just wasting it, is almost like taking poison while being fully aware of the consequences of doing so. It is very wrong for people to feel deeply sad when they lose some money, while when they waste the precious moments of their lives they do not have the slightest feeling of regret. Such an indifference comes as a result of not realizing the value and rarity of the precious human existence. Therefore, you should determine that on the basis of this precious human existence you have the capability and capacity to undertake the practice of dharma.

DIFFICULTY OF ATTAINING HUMAN EXISTENCE

In the next phase, you should reflect upon the difficulty of obtaining a human existence in the future. You should reflect upon the rarity of obtaining a human form from the point of view of its causes: how only through the aggregation of many factors can one achieve it. Compared to other forms of existence and life, human existence and life are very rare and difficult to find.

When you reflect upon the rarity of the precious human form, you might have the feeling that although this human existence has great potential, since you are already quite old it might be better to hope to obtain a better human existence in a future life and embark then upon the path when you are much younger. But it is very difficult to say whether or not you will succeed in obtaining a precious human existence in the future. Such an attitude is almost like that of a person who, when having money with him, spends it without any consideration and purpose, just hoping that he will get more in the future and be able to do business with it. Such a person is stupid. By comparison, a person who, even though he might have a very small amount of money, preserves it and builds on it and does whatever business he wants to with it is a more intelligent person. Similarly, you should use the present potential of the human body already at hand, rather than hope for the future.

Unlike other forms of life, such as elephants, however old we might be we are able to recite at least a mantra and are able to ponder upon questions of karma and its results and our future lives and so forth. There is still potential within us to make progress.

Now, how do we reflect on the rarity of attaining a human existence? First of all, I think it is very important to have some understanding of the Buddhist view of dependent origination. How do we determine whether or not something exists? This is done on the basis of whether or not a phenomenon is established by a certifying consciousness, a valid cognizer. Within the category of existent phenomena, there are some that exist occasionally. The occasional nature of their existence is a sign that they depend upon other factors, causes, and conditions for their arisal; therefore, they are other-powered. The other type is that of permanent phenomena which do not depend on causes and conditions for their existence.

The first category of phenomena consists of dependent phenomena, and within this category there are external phenomena like matter, and others that are only in the nature of clarity and knowing, which are known as consciousnesses. Then there are others such as time, which are abstract phenomena—although they exist, they are not tangible like material phenomena. So, we find that there are three categories of dependent phenomena.

Since we are concerned with the phenomena that directly relate to our experience of pain and pleasure, we are here concerned with the phenomena that are related to consciousness. One can never talk about pain and pleasure as isolated from consciousness. Here it is important to reflect on the causality of phenomena that are related to our inner faculty, mind and consciousness. It is very obvious to us that the body, which is the basis for our experience of pain and pleasure, is in the nature of suffering and is dependent upon causes and conditions. Then, we possess the faculty called consciousness; it exists, it is the agent through which we experience pain and pleasure, but it does not possess any form, color, or anything. Yet this mysterious force is there.

Just as the external body has causes and conditions, the inner faculty, consciousness, also has causes and conditions. When we reflect in such terms, we will be able to see that within the causes there are two types: substantial causes that eventually turn into their fruits, and cooperative causes that contribute to the production of particular fruits. Phenomena possess certain essential qualities—for example, the wetness of water and the heat of fire—which are their natural defining characteristics. These characteristics cannot be said to be produced by a specific cause. I do not know if the karmic forces of sentient beings can affect these natural characteristics.

We find that within phenomena there are certain laws: natural laws, the laws of dependence, functional laws, and the laws of logical evidence. The first one, the law of nature, is very important as a basis; first of all, it is very important to recognize the basic nature of a phenomenon. For example, the basic nature of a consciousness is clarity and knowing. After having perceived the basic nature of a consciousness on the basis of such knowledge, one will be able to understand it better. Understanding that the basic element of matter is atoms will be likewise helpful.

I think that there are some parallels between the disciplines of modern science—physics, chemistry, etc.—and some of the Buddhist concepts. Matter possesses certain natural characteristics, and consciousness possesses certain characteristics as well. The *Kalachakra Tantra* speaks of space particles as the source of all matter, from which later evolves this entire universe; eventually, all matter will be dissolved back into the space particles. I do not know whether or not one can posit a beginning or an end to these subtle particles. But in *Chatu-shataka Shastra* (The Four Hundred Verses), Aryadeva does say that although lacking a beginning, matter does possess an end. So, if we trace the matter that we see on this earth to its source, we will find that it is originally in the form of potential in these space particles.

When we reflect in such terms, we will be able to see a basic law of inter-dependence within all these phenomena. Nevertheless, it is very difficult to speak fully about all the subtle aspects of these laws. Buddhist philosophy speaks of the extremely subtle aspect of karmic law, the law of causality, as an object of knowledge only for the omniscient mind, and perceptible only by the wisdom of a fully enlightened being.

All the phenomena that are directly related to our experience of pain and pleasure—of the body, environment, and so forth—due to their causal conditions increase and decrease and go through the process of change. Among these phenomena there are certain ones that go through the process of change naturally, and others, such as the experiences of happiness and suffering, that go through certain changes when the being interacts with external conditions.

In order to achieve a human existence in the future with a precious body, the causes and conditions that bring about such a result should also be precious, because there should be a concordance between causes and their effects. Just as the result is very rare, similarly the causes themselves are very rare. So the appropriate cause for obtaining a human existence in the future, as the text here discusses, is to have a very proper foundation of a practice of morality—at minimum an abstaining from the ten negative actions.[23] In addition to this basis, the practice of generosity, patience, and so on are also required, which will contribute to the positive qualities of human existence such as having a better intelligence, and so forth. These complementing factors should themselves be complemented by aspirational prayers dedicated to the obtaining of such a human form conducive to the practice of dharma. So, you need these three factors: the foundation, the complementing practices, and a strong force of aspiration to obtain such a body.

If we were to examine whether or not we possess within us these causes that have the potential and power to bring about a human existence in the future, we would find that achieving such an existence is very difficult, very rare, for us. Most of us are so habituated to negative actions and emotions that virtuous thoughts come about only accidentally or through great effort. We are not as accustomed to them as we are to negative actions, which flow like a stream of water running downhill. Because of the habit of our minds, the arisal of negative emotions is effortless for us, whereas the arisal of virtuous thoughts is very difficult—we really have to work to generate them, as though we were driving a donkey up hill. If we consider matters in such terms, we will find that our own minds are always tormented by negative thoughts and that these impulses lead us to negative actions. If this is what happens when we are born as human beings and are equipped with the knowledge to discriminate between right and wrong, what would it be like if we were born in the lower realms, as animals for example, and were not equipped with such knowledge or intelligence?

If we think in such terms, we will be able to infer that we must have accumulated great stores of non-virtues and negativities in past lives. If we were to recollect our own past actions even in this lifetime, we would find that we have indulged in more negative actions than positive. If such is the case with this present life, there is no need to say what kind of actions we must have committed in past lives.

Furthermore, the negative actions in which we have indulged are really very complete from all points of view. For example, when we kill a mosquito or a bug, we have the intention to kill it, we use the most severe means to kill it, and then at the end we rejoice that we have killed it. So, even one negative action has a very strong motivation, an action, and also a sense of satisfaction at the end. This is not the case with positive actions. Besides, negative actions have the potential to increase, whereas positive actions can be destroyed by many adverse circumstances. For example, although we may have accumulated great stores of merit by making prostrations and so forth, if we generate strong anger, this anger—even though it might be momentary—will just blow away a large part of the merit that we might have accumulated yesterday. We will then have to start all over again.

We find that it is very rare that we engage in positive actions. Even those that are accumulated are very weak and also very vulnerable to the effects of negative actions. In view of this, it is important to study the texts that speak of the great advantage of reflecting upon emptiness; even a slight understanding of emptiness, be it just a wavering thought, can destroy great stores of negative karma. This is very true, and reflection on it will give us encouragement to accumulate merit.

Judge whether or not you possess these causes within you for obtaining a precious human life in the future. If you develop a certainty that you possess these factors within you, then there is no need to request or seek others' help, because you possess all the necessary conditions within you. But if you lack these basic factors, then, even though you might invoke the power and inspiration of other forces, it is very doubtful that you will be helped.

When you do the meditation, reflect upon the rarity of the precious human existence first by using all kinds of analogies (though it is very difficult to find an analogy that can totally illustrate the great potential of human existence), and then by considering it in terms of its own nature, and finally by thinking about the rarity of its causes. This order of reflection on the rarity of the precious human existence of leisure and fortune is said to have great significance and has been recommended by many great masters of the past.

If you think in such terms, you will be able to convince yourself that you should make the effort and take the initiative right now when you have obtained a human life. So, make whatever effort you can, now that you have a human body. Make the decision to undertake dharma practice right now in this very life. With that, the reflection on the great significance and rarity of human life is over, and you should affirm this by again visualizing nectar descending and so forth.

These reflections help persuade us from within to engage in the practice of dharma, and thus are preliminary factors. Next follows the actual path. This is divided into three: training the mind in the stages of the path common to the practitioners of initial capacity, training the mind in the stages of the path common to the middling capacity, and training the mind in the stages of the path of the great capacity.

3 Death and Impermanence

The essence of the reflection on death and impermanence can be condensed into a verse from the *Chatu-shataka Shastra*:

> Unwholesome deeds should be reversed first,
> And then in the middle, the "self."
> Later eliminate all erroneous views.
> He who knows such a sequence is wise.

You should develop the conviction that awareness of death and impermanence is an important element of the Buddha's teaching, and that this is why the Buddha taught impermanence at the beginning of all his teachings when he first taught the Four Noble Truths.

The first phase of the practice is to restrain the negative actions that could propel you to lower realms of existence. The cause of your body is contaminated actions and delusions, and as long as you are under their influence there is no place for happiness. In a similar way there is no possibility of happiness and peace while someone is under the leadership of a very negative person. Therefore, reflect upon the fact that you are under the rule of ignorance; ignorance is like the despotic king, and anger and attachment are like his ministers. We live under the tyranny and influence of ignorance, the self-grasping attitude, and also the self-cherishing attitude—factors that all the buddhas and bodhisattvas treat as real enemies. The worst thing is to be under the influence and grip of these negative factors; therefore in the second chapter of *Pramanavartika* (A Thorough Explanation of Valid Cognitions), Dharmakirti says that from the reflection on impermanence one will be able to lead oneself on to the realization of the suffering nature.

The second phase is to engage in the method of rooting out the delusions that are the root of these negative actions. This is done by applying their opponent force, the wisdom realizing emptiness, which eliminates the grasping at self-existence. Eliminating these delusions, together with their root, marks the achievement of liberation.

The third phase is to eliminate the dispositions or imprints left by the delusions that obstruct you from achieving omniscience, the direct knowledge of all phenomena. This should be done by complementing the wisdom realizing emptiness with the factors of method—compassion, bodhicitta, patience, generosity and so forth. If you are able to cultivate a powerful mind that focuses on the welfare of infinite numbers of sentient beings, you will develop a courage that is able to endure infinite hardships for their benefit. Because of the great power of this practice, you will be able to accumulate great stores of merit. When you accumulate these stores of merit by complementing the wisdom of emptiness with the powerful factor of method, you will be able to free yourself totally from all wrong views and misconceptions.

Even in ordinary terms, you would need to have a certain fear of impending danger in order to seek a refuge. Similarly, in order to have a firm practice of refuge, it is first very important to recognize the danger that you are facing. Doing this depends upon a recognition of the unsatisfactory and pain-producing nature of life in this cyclic existence. When you have clearly recognized the frustrating nature of life in this cycle of existence in general, and the sufferings in the lower realms in particular, a genuine desire to seek refuge will follow. To achieve such a recognition, some reflection on impermanence and death is essential. Therefore, when the Buddha taught the Four Noble Truths, he first spoke of impermanence. This is what is explained in the first chapter of *The Four Hundred Verses*; although the actual words are difficult to understand, the text deals extensively with the general and specific sufferings of cyclic existence.

The practical commentaries list the practices that help us overcome attraction to the affairs of this lifetime as follows: understanding the advantages of reflecting on death and impermanence; contemplating the disadvantages of not doing so; and the actual meditation on death, performed by mimicking the death experience.

Gungthang Tenpai Dronme said in his *Mitag Gomtsul Gyi Labjha* (Advice on How to Meditate on Impermanence):

> The thoughts that in this year and month
> I will put right all my tasks and plans
> And then start a perfect dharma practice
> Is in fact the devil which brings all downfalls.

The lack of death awareness prevents one from undertaking the practice of dharma. This is very true: If one is not aware of the eventuality of death, one will be totally concerned and preoccupied with the affairs of this lifetime alone, and with actions that are just for the benefit of this lifetime. Such ventures may take all one's time and energy, but no matter how important they appear to be, since they are directly related to this lifetime alone, their benefits are limited—once one leaves the present body, their benefit ends. Even though one might have a best friend, when one has to leave the body, one cannot take the friend along.

So many people have been born in this world in the past, but all of them are now just memories. Just as the texts say, great buddhas and bodhisattvas of the past, although great beings, also are only memories. The same is true of great kings and so forth. Reflect upon the fact that even the Buddha himself has passed into nirvana. The same will happen to us. Think of how things will look after one hundred years: none of the people assembled now inside this temple will be alive. Even this building may not remain. To prove this, it is not necessary to quote from scriptures nor to give any logical reasons. Even since last year's teachings, I can see that some of my friends have passed away. The same will happen to those who have gathered here this year—next year when we gather for the teachings it is definite that some of us will be no more—but none of us will even have the thought, "It will be me," because of our strong habituation to the apprehension of permanence.

Think that after twenty or thirty years even the Dalai Lama, who has been talking so much, will also be no more. While I am alive, there will be people who are, from the depths of their hearts, prepared to give their lives for my sake, but on the day when I have to leave, I cannot take even one among them with me. Neither will I be able to take any of my possessions, even the body which has been with me since the time of my birth and which I have always preserved and protected. This also will be left behind. At that time of my death, what will benefit is only the positive seeds that are imprinted upon my consciousness. No other factors will help at that time. This is very true, a fact that can be proved and observed.

Therefore, if you are totally concerned and preoccupied with the affairs of this lifetime, there is a great danger of causing your own downfall. If by such concern you were able to achieve the desired happiness, that is okay, but this is not the case. We all let ourselves be caught in this web of preoccupation with the activities and confusion of this lifetime. Having too much worldly involvement ends in confusion. We spend our whole lives thinking that this might be better than that, I should do this, or perhaps something else is better and I should do that. If you reflect upon the underlying dissatisfaction, then you will be able to find that, well, after all, whatever they might be, the affairs of this lifetime are not that important, because they yield a limited benefit. This does not mean that you should not work for your own livelihood, but it does indicate that you should not be preoccupied with that alone.

Your meditation on death and impermanence should be inspired by great delight. You should see this meditation as a factor that will really encourage you to engage in dharma practice.

If you have the awareness of death you stand to gain a lot. It is important not only at the initial stage, but also during the actual path. When you possess such awareness and mindfulness, although you may work for your own livelihood, you will not take that as the most important thing. If a person has prepared for death from a long time back, when death comes it will not come as a shock because he will be well prepared; he will feel that death is merely like changing his clothes. Whereas if a person just avoids the question of death, trying to forget about it, then when death comes, he might be caught totally unprepared and be bewildered by it. When some of my friends who have little interest in the dharma and who have become very old are told that they might die soon—as is obvious—they are not able to actually endure such statements, and so people deceive them by giving them a false feeling that they are going to live long.

We find that the lives of some people who were connected to the fate of the Tibetans—such as Mao Tse Tung and Stalin— have not in the end been quite admirable. Such people have meted out a lot of destruction and have not been able to accomplish even the negative actions that they set out to do. They have had to live their whole lives under great anxiety and pressure. This is an obvious fact.

But if you are mindful of death and have this death awareness, you will always think of the future and make preparations for it, and when death strikes it will not come as a surprise, so you will not be so anxious. Consequently, at that point you will be able to maintain your calmness of mind.

Just requesting prayers from others at the time of death and not doing anything yourself is very improper and contradicts any claim that you are a follower of dharma. Sometimes I actually say this when people come to seek my prayers for them. I know an old Tibetan lady who always used to ask me, "Oh,

Your Holiness, do not let me fall in the hell realms"—as though I have that in my hand! There is nothing I can do if she has done nothing on her part. Not only I, but even the Buddha does not have the power to save such a being. Therefore, the Buddha taught the infallibility of karmic law. If the great beings like the Buddha have the power to determine the fate of the living beings, then there is no need for him to talk about the infallibility of karmic law. If you are equipped with this death awareness, you will always work to accumulate virtuous actions to prepare for your future.

To do the actual meditation on death, you should reflect on the certainty of death and the unpredictability of its time, and that at the time of death it is only dharma that can benefit you. Meditation on the certainty of death is undertaken through reasoning on three facts: that death definitely comes and no circumstances can prevent it; that life ebbs away uninterruptedly and cannot be extended; and that time is scarce for dharma practice even while one is alive. With these contemplations, you must decide to practice dharma. After meditating on the certainty of death, consider the fact that the lifetime of living beings on this planet is very unpredictable, and therefore death might strike any time. Reflecting on its unpredictability will persuade you to undertake the practice of dharma with a note of urgency. So, with that, you should make a decision to practice right now. Then reflect that at the time of death, wealth, possessions, friends, relatives, and even your own body will not be beneficial. With this, you should decide to only practice dharma.

The oral instruction says that after meditating on the certainty of death, it is effective to contemplate the death process, mimicking the actual situation. How do you do that? Just imagine how a dying person feels at the time of death. The doctors abandon you and you find yourself lost. If you are suffering from chronic illness, the doctors will have lost hope and the relatives or friends will seek the prayers of spiritual beings. On your own part, you will have to face the situation. You will be unable to move your body from the mattress and you will wear the last clothes; and even though you might want to leave some message, it is very difficult even to speak the words that you want to say. It is even doubtful whether or not you will have the time to give this message. And then the last food that you take will be, for a religious practitioner, blessed pills and so forth, though you may not be able to swallow them. It is difficult to know if you can gain much from pinning all your hopes on taking some blessed pills. But still, it is human nature to keep hoping.

As you are dying, you will have all sorts of illusions when the physical elements within your body begin to dissolve and lose their force. Often these dissolution processes are associated with frightening experiences and hallucinations. At that time, you will become more and more distant from what is called the present life, for the sake of which you have indulged in all kinds of negative actions. You might also have indications of your future fate, having all sorts of illusions or hallucinations of fires or water, of being submerged underground or feeling heaviness of the body, and so forth. Gradually, even the breath will lose its force; eventually the breathing will grow faint. Finally, you will just exhale and not be able to inhale, and at that point, just like a fiddle string breaking, your link to the present body comes to an end.

At that time, you will be known as the late so and so. The very name—Tenzin and so forth—that might have inspired pleasure and happiness in relatives before, will now need a prefix, "late."

That marks the end of a life. It is effective to reflect upon this process. It is very descriptively explained in the writings of Gungthang Jamphelyang and Phabongkha Dechen Nyingpo, whose texts are very helpful. To quote a few verses from Phabongkha's *Mitag Drenkul Nyingi Thurma* (Reminder of Impermanence):

> Though you eagerly prepare yourself,
> With constant thoughts of many morrows,
> The time will come when you will be forced

To leave right now and here.
The time will come when you will leave
Without any control, with things unfinished:
Tasks, meals and even half-finished drinks.

The time will come when you will pull
From the clothes and hands of your friends,
With hands very weak and feeble,
While lying down and unable to move,
On your last mattress, which you can use only today,
As though an old tree has fallen.

The time will come when you will see
Your own corpse for the first time,
When your body becomes hard as a rock,
Though wrapped in and out with your last bedding,
Clothing which you can use only today.

The time will come when you will be overwhelmed
By depressions and frustrations
From being unable to communicate with others
Through your last words of death-will and complaints,
Spoken with a dry mouth though with all the effort.

With this, the contemplation on death and impermanence
is over.

4 Sufferings of the Lower Realms

The next meditation of the practitioners of initial capacity is the reflection upon the sufferings of the lower realms. Again focusing upon the spiritual master, you should reflect that when your link to this present life ends, there are only two possibilities for your future existence: the favorable and unfavorable forms of existence.

As we discussed earlier, the end of birth is death, and at that point the present body ceases. Among the many different consciousnesses, there are coarser ones, such as the sensory consciousnesses, which are very dependent upon the body. All these consciousnesses have a basic nature, which is the Clear Light; there is no possibility of consciousness originating from a cause that is not in the nature of Clear Light. So this Clear Light mind is known as the fundamental innate consciousness, and when it interacts with circumstances, external factors, it produces the grosser levels of mind.

Because the continuity of this subtle form of consciousness is beginningless, it is possible sometimes—even for ordinary people—to recall the death experiences of the past. I know some Indian children who are able to recall very clearly and vividly their past lives, the circumstances under which they had to die, and the experiences they went through at the time of death.

Such remembrance is a phenomenon that one can observe now. Some people, when they subdue the active forces of the gross levels of mind as a result of their meditations, are able to increase the force of the subtle levels of consciousness through the experience of Clear Light. As a result of such experiences, they are able to recall their past lives vividly. This shows that there are events in the past that are objects of our recollection and memory, which indicates that there are past lives.

There is no factor that can end the continuity of this consciousness, which is in the nature of clarity and knowing. At death time, consciousness has to separate from the present body and undergo the intermediate state. At that point, one experiences a subtle form of consciousness—this does not refer to the subtle forms of consciousness developed as a result of meditation. There are many different levels of consciousness; when the mind is withdrawn from active attention to external objects, one is able to abandon the grosser levels and experience a subtle level.

There are three levels of consciousness; the experiences of these different consciousnesses result in different levels of existence. The lowest is the realm of desire, where the level of mind is very gross and where people are more attracted to external objects. Next comes the form realm, with its sixteen divisions, where the mind is subtler and more withdrawn from external objects. Then there is a realm known as the formless realm, which is divided into four. It is a state of existence that is temporarily free not only from suffering and dissatisfaction but also from ordinary feelings of joy and pleasure, experiences that normally result in desire and discontent. Although it is very difficult to logically prove the existence of these levels, you can judge that the states of mind that you have could result in different states of existence in the future. The nature of these can be inferred by judging the quality of our mind and the degree to which it is dominated by desire, hatred, anger, and so forth.

After death, the individual takes rebirth in any of the three realms of existence, which are broadly classified into two: the favorable and the unfavorable migrations, also known as the higher and lower rebirths. The favorable transmigrations include birth as a celestial being (of a formless, form or desire realm), an *asura* (demi-god) or a human being. The unfavorable transmigrations include rebirth as an animal, a wandering spirit or a hell being.

I do not know if the hell realms really do exist as described so vividly in the Abhidharma literature, yet one thing that is obvious is that the environment is very much associated with the beings living therein. In our case, we are deeply interdependent with the planet earth, which is our natural habitat. However, this delicate interdependence was not understood by mankind in the past, and this unfortunately has led human beings to take many things too much for granted. This ignorance has resulted in an immoral exploitation of the planet, with a devastating effect on both the environment and the lives within it. If we examine our planet and the lives on it, we will be amazed to find much evidence suggesting an underlying balance at the basis of all. Consider how differing trees have appropriate features that give them the capacity to multiply their class and thus survive. For example, some trees have flowers with cotton-like covers which can be blown away by the wind so the species can survive. If we were to reflect upon the individual causes of all these distinctions, it would be difficult to explain everything logically. The same is true of living beings: the fact that all the living beings have gone through the evolutionary process in this world for more than five billion years is really very profound and difficult to believe. It is not surprising, since that is the case, that descriptions of other forms of life on other planets and so forth are difficult to understand, but that does not mean that such forms do not exist.

Therefore, since living beings are infinite and have all sorts of forms, shapes and colors, one can infer that also their environments, their natural habitats, could be totally different from ours. Buddhist writings speak of numberless systems of universes. Modern scientific cosmology comes close to the Buddhist explanation of infinite universal systems, but the particular description that we find in Abhidharma and also some sutras, such as *Do-de Drenpa Nyershag* (Sutra on Mindfulness), may not be taken as literal. The logical explanations of the specific causes of the diverse shapes, physical compositions, colors and so forth of the countless universal systems are very hidden from us, as are the subtlest aspects of karma and their results.

There are various sufferings in the lower realms. Those realms of existence where the experience of suffering is most intense are categorized as the hell realms; that where confusion and ignorance are most powerful is regarded as the realm of animals, where the powerful devour the weak; that where the sufferings of hunger and thirst are most acute is viewed as the realm of *pretas* (hungry ghosts).

You should reflect on what it would be like to take rebirth in a lower form of existence—as a dog, for example. Just imagine how you would feel and what could be your fate! One is not born in these lower realms without any cause, merely by accident. When the causes and conditions for such a rebirth have been aggregated, birth into such realms naturally follows. Reflect upon the fact that if you have accumulated the causes such as stealing, killing, etc.—if these actions are very strong and forceful—then the fruition of these actions would be rebirth in the hell realms. Actions that were a little less forceful would throw you into rebirth as a hungry ghost, and those somewhat milder would give you rebirth as an animal.

Since it is certain that we all have accumulated all sorts of negative actions within this lifetime, our undergoing experience of these lower realms is only a matter of time. The moment the process of breathing ends, our future life begins. Reflecting in such terms, not just observing but rather mimicking the situation, imagining that you are undergoing these sufferings will be powerful and effective.

Do this contemplation, as the Fifth Dalai Lama's *Lamrim* and Lama Tsongkhapa's *Lamrim Chenmo* recommend, by imagining that you are undergoing such sufferings to the degree that you develop a kind of fear and a feeling of unbearableness. If you find these experiences unbearable, realize that you have the opportunity right now to prevent yourself from falling into the lower realms. Reflect upon the factors that cause one to take rebirth in such realms of existence, checking within your mind whether or not you have the causes and conditions for lower rebirth, or have committed them in the past, or are committing them right now, or may commit them in the future. Then strive for the means to eliminate them. Make a request prayer to the spiritual master that you may never indulge in these negative actions. The actual means of protecting yourself from the danger of falling into the lower realms of existence is to bring about the realization of the dharma within your mind.

Some people might feel that if they actually meet with the experiences of the lower realms they will face them, but since they are not undergoing such experiences right now, it is pointless to mimic them and imagine undergoing them. This is not a practical outlook. Generally speaking, it is the way of a courageous person to take precautionary measures and be prepared before an eventuality strikes. But just waiting for something to happen and not being prepared is the way of a fool. Having generated a genuine feeling of unbearableness for the sufferings in the lower realms of existence by imagining the experience of being born there, and also by realizing the presence of causes within yourself for taking rebirth in such realms, you undertake a new initiative to seek immunity from such a danger. The actual preventative measure is to take, from the depths of your heart, refuge in the Three Jewels, and to respect the karmic law of causality.

5 *Seeking Refuge*

The next phase is the practice of taking refuge and developing deep conviction in the law of causality.

In order to have a very firm and reinforced practice of refuge, you can visualize the objects of refuge. This is done by visualizing light rays emanating from the heart of the spiritual master at your heart. Then again visualize buddhas and bodhisattvas in front of you in the space above. Reflect upon their exceptional qualities of body, speech and mind, and think that you have experienced the intense sufferings of the lower realms in the past, and if you do not control yourself at this time you might continue to undergo such suffering in the future as well. With such reflection, you should entrust yourself totally to the care of these objects of refuge and seek refuge in them. Then visualize nectar descending, which purifies the negativities.

To explain in brief, taking refuge is the factor that determines whether or not one is a Buddhist. Therefore, it is the entrance into the Buddhist community, marks one's becoming a Buddhist, and lays a proper foundation for taking subsequent vows. Its practice can take various forms. There are some forms of refuge practice that are based on a reasoned conviction derived through valid cognition. Those who may not have such a faculty but who have seen and admired the great qualities and capacities of the Buddha, dharma and sangha, can—on the basis of their personal convictions—take them as an infallible refuge. The Buddha said in one sutra:

> Faith is the forerunner of all positive deeds,
> Hence should be cultivated first;
> It safeguards all virtuous qualities,
> And enhances them as well.

The more progress you make in your spiritual path and the more advanced you become, the better your practice of refuge can become. Someone who possesses this factor of refuge entrusts himself or herself totally to the care and guidance of the Three Jewels and takes refuge in them. To have a successful practice of refuge, it is first of all necessary to cultivate the two basic causes for seeking refuge, which are the factors of fear and conviction, as discussed earlier.

Just reflect that it is your natural tendency to wish to experience happiness and avoid suffering, and that you can accomplish this feat by cultivating the dharma within yourself. What is meant by dharma is the spiritual realization that you can achieve as a result of your practice. Any factor that can enable you to achieve total liberation from delusions and sufferings and bring about the realization of a true cessation is the true dharma. Since delusions do not reside in the essential nature of the mind, they are adventitious and can be purged and cleared away from your mind when the right opponent forces are applied. Once you are able to free yourself totally and get rid of the delusions which are the causes of your sufferings, then there is no possibility of experiencing sufferings. The achievement of that liberation marks total victory, and that is true cessation, or in other words, the dharma. Cessation of suffering and delusions does not refer to delusions becoming exhausted through the passage of time, but rather it refers to a state where one has achieved a form of cessation developed through one's applying the actual opponent forces that destroy the potential of delusion within. That "cessation" is dharma, so when one says, "Dharma is refuge," one should have the understanding that dharma is the path that leads one to the state of liberation and also the state of cessation itself, and that these are the actual refuge.

The moment someone has these realizations, such a person is regarded as a superior being or an *arya*. All people employing skillful means, if they are able to free themselves from delusions and sufferings and achieve their cessation, are spiritual beings and form the spiritual community.

Because seeing such spiritual persons can be encouraging, spiritual communities are helpful. We beginners require the companionship of the spiritual community. By leaning on the support of some superior persons, we are able to make progress. Such people possess the realizations and cessations and, due to their experience, are able to guide us properly. Even for worldly knowledge we require teachers.

We need the guidance of a fully accomplished master who is able to lead us on the right path to the achievement of cessation, through a gradual process and in the proper order of the path, because cessation is a state that can be achieved only through a gradual process—it cannot come about instantly. Therefore, it is very important to rely upon a spiritual master or the Buddha, the master of the doctrine, a master who possesses the compassion that is totally impartial and encompasses all sentient beings within its sphere. Lama Tsongkhapa said:

> Those who are outside your doctrine,
> Though they persevere with hardships for long,
> Strengthen the view grasping at self,
> As though hastily asking for miseries.

Masters of other religious disciplines are admirable because their teachings benefit many people, but since Buddhist practitioners are engaged in a path leading to the ultimate liberation and are not confined to the perfection of this lifetime alone, they should have a unique master conforming to their own mode of spiritual path. Generally speaking, all the masters of the major religious of this world should be respected and should be admired, be they Buddhist or non-Buddhist. At the same time, when it comes to our own refuge, it is important to go for refuge to the Buddha. It is not a question of being partial, because it is only someone who has realized the real meaning of emptiness who will be able to show the path leading to liberation through experience and the doctrine which outline the path leading to liberation through experience.

The importance and significance of the master Buddha come from the nature of the dharma. As I remarked earlier, understanding of dharma can be developed on the basis of understanding the Two Truths and the Four Noble Truths. Let us take a phenomenon, a single object; although it has many levels of characteristics and qualities, it is not necessary for one to realize all of them at one time. Similarly, there are many different levels of understanding of the Four Noble Truths. It is only by understanding the subtle views of the Madhyamika Prasangika that one can understand the Four Noble Truths on their subtlest level, but that does not mean one cannot develop an understanding of the Four Noble Truths without these views.

If you understand the dharma, you will be able to respect the other Jewels, too. The word *Kanchok* (Jewel) will have a special meaning. Dharma is very rare and precious; the same is true of the spiritual community and the master of the doctrine. Through such reflections, you will be able to develop a deep conviction that the Jewels are unfailing and reliable when a refuge is sought in them. Having visualized the Three Jewels, it is very effective to reflect upon the exceptional qualities of the master of the doctrine, the Buddha. As mentioned in the opening verse of *Pramana-samucca* (Compendium of Valid Cognitions) by Dignaga, the Buddha is someone who evolved as a fully enlightened being through the perfection of universal compassion and wisdom, hence attaining all the realizations and cessations. Thus we see that great compassion and wisdom are the chief qualities of the Buddha. Even in worldly terms, the more intelligent and knowledgeable a person is, the more the person commands respect. Similarly, the more compassionate, kind and gentle a person, the more he or she should be respected. This is not a matter of religion alone, for not only human beings but even small insects have the natural instinct to be happy and to avoid sufferings, and thus appreciate kindness. So if you are able to develop that intelligence and altruism to their fullest extent, then you are truly admirable and deserve to be respected.

By reflecting upon the great qualities and capacities of the objects of refuge, you will develop a conviction that will be firmly rooted in and deeply based on reason, and thereby able to withstand logical analysis. You should not believe in the preciousness and sanctity of a spiritual being or Buddha just because someone said that this being possesses these qualities; rather you should develop faith and conviction through your own analytic process, by comparing these beings to other masters of doctrine. A refuge practice developed through such a process will be very firm and stable, whereas a practice developed just by relying on a few words of a person will not be very stable. Such a practice will be very much like the Chinese description of Buddhist practice—blind faith.

The attitude of entrusting yourself from the round orb of your heart to a superior being is the proper refuge. It should be deeply felt, and you should entrust yourself totally to the care of the Three Jewels. A recitation of the refuge formula—"I go for refuge to the Buddha"—induced by such a force of mind marks the taking of refuge.

Let us set aside for a while the question of meditational deities, dharmapalas, heroes, and so forth as objects of refuge; the basic necessity is the recognition of the Three Jewels. Now, when the Buddha is spoken of in the context of the Mahayana, you should understand that the reference is not confined to the historical person alone. If it were, then many inconsistencies in the Mahayana writings would emerge. It is very difficult to explain how an ordinary person became totally enlightened within one lifetime without ever practicing highest yoga tantra. Within the Mahayana context, Buddha Shakyamuni should be seen as the *nirmanakaya* (emanation body), the attainment of which, one assumes, is possible only when a being has achieved the *sambhogakaya* (enjoyment body). Both these bodies are dependent on the attainment of the *dharmakaya* (truth body). So an understanding of these three bodies—dharmakaya, sambhogakaya and nirmanakaya—is very important.

Then you should reflect upon the exceptional qualities of the Buddha's great compassion, wisdom, and capacity—in other words, the qualities of his body, speech, mind, activities and so forth. Then you will be able to develop a deep conviction in the buddhas' capacities, because they are the beings who have totally conquered all forms of obstacles and limitations within their minds and who have the ability to enable others to do so. The full meaning of the word *buddha*—fully enlightened—could come about only on the basis of an understanding of the indivisible union of method and wisdom. Only when you develop an understanding of the Buddha in such a manner can the meditational deity become really significant and mean something profound, because realization of a meditational deity is possible only on the basis of undertaking a practice that is a union of method and wisdom. The same is true of protectors, heroes, heroines, dakinis, and so forth, who provide assistance on the path. If you do not have such a firm understanding, perhaps it is better to have just the understanding of Buddha Shakyamuni in his bhikshu form. If your understanding of a meditational deity is not much different from your perception of a non-Buddhist deity, then it is not very profound. Without a proper understanding, visualization of all these complex deities can be more harmful than beneficial.

First, make a fervent request to the spiritual master at your crown to enable you to have the perfect realization of the practice of refuge. As a Mahayanist, you should also wish that all sentient beings may develop the same aspiration. As explained in the section on relying on a spiritual master, do the visualization of the merit field according to your own mental disposition.

At this point, it is very effective to reflect upon the exceptional qualities of the path, starting from the *sravaka*[24] level, first reflecting upon the realization of the sravaka on the path of accumulation[25]: his force of wisdom, meditative stabilization, morality and so forth. You will be able to see that these forces increase on the higher path, eventually leading to the completely enlightened state. Then you will be able to understand the unsurpassable quality of buddhahood, as explained in *Ratnavali, Uttaratantra, Madhyamikavatara, Abhisamayalankara*, and similar texts. This understanding will help you to develop a very strong conviction and faith in the Buddha. Reflect that although all sentient beings have these objects of refuge, if they do not realize their great significance and capacity, then how can they take refuge in them? As a result, they are tormented and plunged into the confusion of cyclic existence. Pray that, from now on, just as you undertake the practice of refuge, may all sentient beings equally have such realizations.

After having undertaken the practice of refuge, you should observe the precepts of refuge, the abandonments and the affirmations. All these precepts should be studied from *Lamrim Chenmo* by Lama Tsongkhapa. This text is like the constitution; it is very important, and you should study and practice it. *Path to Bliss*, on which you are receiving teachings right now, should be taken as a key with which you can unlock the treasure found in *Lamrim Chenmo*.

As a precept of taking refuge, you should never indulge in the business of selling statues and scriptures for profit, and you should never talk of or judge the value of statues on the basis of their material. Whether they are made of clay or any precious material, they should be treated equally. Also observe the precept of seeing the distinctive features of the Buddhist master and the doctrine. Among all the precepts of taking refuge, the most important is to observe the law of causality, living your life with awareness of the laws of karma.

Also reflect upon the fact that all the Buddha's activities are motivated by his great compassion and that the essence of his doctrine is to be compassionate and to work for others.

The gist of his message to the world is the practice of a kind heart. A kind heart and altruism bring about a positive atmosphere around the person who practices them. Even a gentle dog makes people around it feel comfortable, whereas a very aggressive dog will make people cautious and apprehensive. Such is true also of human beings: when your companions are calm and gentle and warm-hearted, you can rely on them and trust them. Human beings are social animals who depend for their survival on others' cooperation and assistance. So it is better not to have a companion at all than to have one who is very aggressive and harmful. You can never rely on such a person but always have to be suspicious and apprehensive about him or her. And conversely, if your own character and personality is such that all people avoid you, that is very sad. Therefore, a kind heart and compassion are the real sources of peace and happiness; this compassion, when you enhance it to its fullest potential by employing the right skillful means though meditation, marks the realization of a universal compassion. When such a compassion is further complemented by the factors of wisdom and intelligence, then you will achieve a state called buddhahood in which you totally sacrifice yourself for the benefit of others; such a compassion and kind heart are really priceless and most precious.

So, when you have developed a strong force of taking refuge in the Three Jewels, you should, as an expression of your mental attitude, recite the refuge formula. Repeat the recitation, and when you find that you begin to lose the force of your contemplation, leave the repetition for a while and again reinforce your contemplation, reflecting upon the great kindness of the master Buddha and the great qualities of the dharma and so forth. You should undertake your practice in such a manner. Normally, if you have someone in whom you have great confidence and to whom you entrust yourself, you will be able to follow with greater willingness and delight the advice that he gives to you. Similarly, the more you feel confidence in the Three Jewels, particularly the Buddha, the more forceful your refuge in them becomes. You feel closer to a being such as the Buddha and, from the depths of your heart, will be able to have deep conviction and confidence in such a person. As a result, naturally your admiration for that person will increase and you will emulate his noble example. As a result, whenever you are faced with circumstances where you might engage in negative actions, you will naturally restrain yourself from them, thinking, "I should not do that as it is against the ideals of the Buddha and his doctrine, and I am a spiritual person, a bhikshu, so I should refrain from such actions." Such a restraint would eventually extend even to your thoughts in dreams as well. Restraint from negative actions marks the realization of having sought refuge; refuge has reinforced your courage to do positive actions and weakened your boldness to indulge in negative actions.

The root of the Buddha's doctrine is compassion and the practice of non-harming. Since you claim to be a practitioner of this doctrine, you should keep the essential precept of taking refuge in the dharma: never to indulge in actions harmful to others, even to small animals. For example, it is beneficial to save animals who are in danger of being killed. If you can help them, do it, but if not, at least never harm them.

As a precept of taking refuge in the spiritual community, you should not associate yourself with people who are not dharma practitioners. Even someone wearing the smallest patch of yellow robes should be respected. Since the spiritual community is regarded as an object of refuge, its members have a great responsibility to live exemplary lives. On their part, they should make themselves worthy of such respect. It is very important to make the effort. There has never been a being, no matter how great his or her spiritual realizations—Aryadeva or Nagarjuna or even the Buddha himself—who was totally enlightened and free of faults at birth. Just because you have weaknesses and faults, you should not feel discouraged and careless, saying, "I have these faults and cannot help it." Rather, you should feel that you also have the natural notion of "self" that serves as the basis of the instinctive wish to attain happiness and avoid suffering. If you try to transform yourself for the better, there is a possibility of reducing your chances of suffering in the future and increasing your chances for happiness. On the part of the lay community, it is important to respect the spiritual community.

Of all the practices, the most important factor is to have the altruistic attitude, which is the essence of the doctrine. It is also the key to a happy and successful society. You should have a kind heart and never harm others. I say this whenever I meet people, because I have a deep conviction in these principles and find them very effective and beneficial, and think the same will be true for others. If someone lacks a kind heart and the altruistic motivation and internally has a very negative mind, even though he might be a spiritual practitioner like a bhikshu in external appearance, it is most unbecoming. From all perspectives—religious or political or worldly—a kind heart and altruism are like a living jewel, the wish-granting jewel. The meditation on compassion is therefore most important, not only for those who have great knowledge of dharma, but also for those who lack such knowledge.

6 *Karma*

The next meditation is the contemplation on karmic law. The foundation and root of attaining all the perfection of the future is the living of one's life with awareness of the law of causality.

As we discussed earlier, the phenomena that are directly related to our experience of pain and pleasure are subject to the law of interdependence and therefore depend on their causes and conditions. If there is a cause, the effects ensue and themselves in turn become causes and produce their fruits. So there is a kind of chain reaction—it is like playing a snooker game, in which one ball hits another and that hits another and so on. This law of interdependence is very powerful. Things that we would never expect sometimes arise, such as a small cause triggering great change and transformation. That is the meaning of the law of interdependence.

The presentation of the law of causality is the presentation of a natural fact. It can be explained briefly in this way: if you do positive actions, you will face desirable consequences and if you engage in negative actions, you will have to face undesirable consequences. There is a connection of commensuration between cause and effect. Any action that produces happiness is positive. The distinction between negative and positive can be made only by judging the fruits.

Happiness and suffering can be posited only on the basis of the feeling of a living being. If that factor of feeling is not taken into account, what basis can there be for making such a distinction between positive and negative or harm and benefit? Since we have to accept harm and benefit, or in other words pain and pleasure, any causes that give rise to suffering are negative, and any causes that give rise to happiness are positive. Positive actions result in desirable consequences. In this way there is a definiteness in karmic law.

For example, taking the life of another obviously harms the other person. Just as you yourself regard your life as most precious, the same is true of the other person. Therefore, as a result of the action that totally disregards the preciousness of another's life, you will have to face commensurate consequences. It is thus the worst form of negative action. Compared to that, a slightly lesser evil is the stealing of others' belongings. Stealing is harmful to others because it harms their possessions and thus hurts their feelings. Although its consequences may not be as grave as those of taking the life of others, nevertheless, stealing is a negative act, and accordingly you will have to face commensurate consequences.

Sometimes we face certain situations where, although we have done something good for others, we may not be able to reap the consequences within this lifetime. When we are talking about the law of causality, we are not limiting its operation to the confines of this life alone, but rather are taking into account both this lifetime and the future. Occasionally people who do not have a proper knowledge of karmic law say that such and such a person is very kind and religious and so forth, but he always has problems, whereas so and so is very deceptive and negative, frequently indulging in negative actions, but always seems very successful. Such people may think that there is no karmic law at all. There are others who go to the other extreme and become superstitious, thinking that when someone experiences illness, it is all due to harmful spirits. If such a person were the disciple of a Kadampa master, he would be beaten with a stick. It is also possible for very negative people to experience their positive karma ripening immaturely due to the very strong force of negative actions, and thus to exhaust the potentials of their virtuous actions. They experience a relative success in this life, while others who are very serious practitioners, as a result of the force of their practices, bring upon this lifetime the consequences of karmic actions which might have otherwise thrown them into rebirth in lower realms of existence in the future. As a result, they experience more problems and illnesses in this life.

Just resolving not to indulge in a negative action is not enough. It should be accompanied by the understanding that it is for your own benefit and sake that you must live with awareness of the law of karma: if you have accumulated the causes, you will have to face the consequences; if you desire a particular effect, you can work to produce its causes; and if you do not desire a certain consequence, you can avoid engaging in actions that will bring it about. You should reflect upon the law of causality as follows: that there is a definite relation between causes and effects; that actions not committed will never produce an effect; and that once committed, actions will never lose their potentiality simply through the passage of time. So, if you wish to enjoy desirable fruits, you should work for the accumulation of the appropriate causes, and if you want to avoid undesirable consequences, you should not accumulate their causes.

Do not have the notion that karmic law is something laid down by the Buddha. Rather, it is a natural law like any other natural law. Although the very subtle aspects of karmic law are extremely hidden for us and can be inferred only by relying upon scriptural sources, there are certain general aspects of which we can develop an understanding through reasoning.

In order to gain such understanding, it is important first of all to develop a deep conviction and faith in the master Buddha. This cannot be produced just by saying that the Buddha possessed such and such physical qualities and had a very impressive personality and so forth. Rather, if after having subjected his doctrine to analysis, you find his teachings to be authentic, very reliable, and able to withstand any analysis, only then can you develop a deep and unshakable faith in him. You should then be able to see that the Buddha is a being who became enlightened through his perfection of a great compassion developed over a long period of time.

To generate the ascertainment that the perfection of a Buddha comes from such a process, it is vital to understand and develop the deep conviction that consciousness has the potential to increase to a limitless level. A proper understanding of buddhahood depends upon a proper understanding of dharma, and this in turn depends upon an understanding of the Four Truths, the deeper knowledge of which in turn depends upon a knowledge of the Two Truths. If you do not understand the Four Truths, you will not be able to understand the Buddha's doctrine properly, and if you do not have a good understanding of the objects of refuge, then it is very difficult to develop a deep conviction in the validity of the law of causality.

If, due to the force of your ignorance and so forth, you find yourself committing negative actions, you should, equipped with the force of the four powers,[26] immediately purify them. There are different methods of purification, such as reciting mantras, meditating on emptiness, doing prostrations, engaging in deity yoga, making offerings, and particularly on days of religious observance taking the Mahayana vows. But the most important point is to have the factor of regret. Once you have that factor, your practice of purification will be very successful. For developing a deep regret for the negative actions, it is vital to see their destructive nature. Once you have seen that, you will have genuine regret, and this will then lead you to apply the opponent forces and to make a very firm resolve never to indulge in these actions again. For example, if you have a very serious and complex illness, you cannot cure it just by taking a medicine composed of one element; rather, you have to take all sorts of measures. Similarly, you need to apply every measure possible to tame your mind, which is under the influence of ignorance. Anger, hatred and desire are also competing for domination of your mind. There is no possibility of taming your mind by using just one means. All the Buddha's teachings bear on the taming of the mind and the bringing about of discipline within it. Since this work is done by employing all sorts of skillful means, one finds many different approaches in the Buddhist writings.

Motivated as they are by all levels of afflictive emotions and delusions (all rooted in ignorance), negative actions committed through the three doors of body, speech and mind are countless. But they can be broadly classified into ten basic actions, as the Buddha taught. Abstaining from these ten negative actions marks the practice of the ten positive actions. Having properly recognized the ten negative actions, you should reflect upon their destructive nature, and impelled by the strong wish to abandon them, should refrain from doing them. There are three negative actions of body: killing, stealing and sexual misconduct; four of speech: lying, divisive speech, harsh words and senseless gossip; and three of mind: covetousness, harmful intent and holding perverted views. If you have indulged in these negative actions, you will take rebirth in the lower realms of existence as their matured fruit. There are also many other levels of fruits, such as the environmental effects[27] and the perpetuation of negative tendencies in the future.

By reflecting upon the destructive nature of the actions and their undesirable consequences, you should cultivate a strong resolve never to indulge in them and should restrain yourself from engaging in them. That, in essence, lays the proper foundation for the practice of morality. On the basis of such morality, you should undertake the practice. In order to achieve a true cessation, it is first of all very important to abstain from the manifest expressions of these delusions—the negative actions—thus gradually reversing negative tendencies of thought. Observing the morality of refraining from the ten negative actions is taught as a precept of taking refuge. This concludes the practice of training in the first phase, that is, training the mind in the stages of the path common to the practitioners of initial capacity.

7 The Defects of Cyclic Existence in General

As in the case of the earlier meditations, this meditation on the defects of cyclic existence should be preceded by the preliminaries.

As Lama Tsongkhapa said in his *Lamrim Nyamgur*:

If you do not contemplate the truth of suffering—the fallacy of samsara—
The wish to be free of samsara will not arise.
If you do not contemplate the source of suffering—the door to samsara—
You will never discover the means of cutting samsara's root.
Base yourself on renunciation of cyclic existence; be tired of it.
Cherish knowledge of the chains that bind you to the wheel of cyclic existence.

Reflect upon the faults of true suffering and then the faults and destructive nature of true origins of suffering, and thus develop the wish to be free from the cycle of existence. And, as Lama Tsongkhapa explained in *Lamtso Namsum* (The Three

Principal Aspects of the Path), you should overcome the attraction to this life and then rise above preoccupation with future lives. It is best to develop the wish to gain freedom from the cycle of existence by understanding the method of doing so, since a wish to be free from cyclic existence not based on a knowledge of method is not likely to be firm and stable. Such an understanding can be developed by recognizing sufferings as sufferings, identifying their origins, and seeking the path which will lead to their cessation. When you see the possibility and certainty of such cessation, by engaging in a path that leads to it, you should develop the strong wish to achieve liberation.

The training of the mind in the stages of the path common to the middling scope, as discussed earlier, is preceded by a loosening of the force of grasping at self-existence of the person. Eventually, by totally eliminating the self-grasping attitude within your mind, you will be able to achieve the permanent state of peace which is called liberation. Without liberation, even though you might attain temporary relief from the obvious sufferings of the lower realms of existence, thus enjoying worldly perfections, this attainment is only a temporary postponement of the sufferings of the lower realms; the moment you meet with the right or appropriate circumstances, you will again take rebirth in the lower realms of existence. The temporary relief from the lower realms afforded by taking rebirth in favorable states of existence is not only unstable but unreliable as well.

Furthermore, when you probe deeply you will find that no matter how high an existence a realm may be, even though it may be the highest state of existence, as long as it is in this cycle of existence the beings there are in the nature of sufferings, because they have the sufferings of pervasive conditioning and are therefore under the influence or command of contaminated actions and delusions. As long as one is not able to be free from such an influence, there is no place for permanent peace or happiness.

The obvious sufferings that are known as the sufferings of

suffering are manifest sufferings that even animals will be able to recognize as suffering and have the desire to be free from. Generally, the experiences that you normally regard as pleasurable and happy, such as having the physical comfort of good facilities and so forth, if they are examined at a deeper level, will be revealed to be changeable and therefore in the nature of suffering. They provide you with temporary satisfaction; because of that temporary satisfaction you regard them as experiences of happiness. But if you keep on pursuing them, they will again lead to the experience of suffering. Most of these pleasurable experiences are not really happiness in the true sense of the word, but only appear as pleasure and happiness in comparison to the obvious sufferings that you have. Thus, all experiences of suffering can be categorized into three classes or levels of suffering: (1) manifest suffering; (2) suffering of change; and (3) the pervasive suffering of conditioning.

Even though you have attained existence in a higher realm, still you are not totally free of the potential suffering of the three lower realms, and as long as you are under the influence of contaminated actions and delusions you will never have independence or freedom. The very fact that you are under the grip and influence of such negative factors is a suffering enough and a state of misery. If the factors that influence you are positive, it is okay, but the factors that command you and determine and influence your life are negative delusions. The very name *delusion* is frightening—its etymological root is the term *afflictive emotion*. The very name suggests that the moment delusions arise within your mind they afflict you and destroy your happiness and calmness. Therefore, delusions are the genuine enemies—you should never hesitate to deal forcefully with them. Delusions reside within your mind in such a manner that they do not feel any threat from you. As long as you totally entrust yourself to their command, there is no prospect for happiness or goodness.

If the enemy is external, there is a possibility of avoiding it; there are also methods of overcoming that enemy by seeking others' help. But if the enemy is within, it is quite difficult to overcome. There is no way that you can avoid it, so it is only by taking the initiative yourself and making the effort that you will be able to combat it. You should therefore determine that taking the initiative is important on your part, and that there is no chance of freeing yourself from the grip of delusions if you do not seek the means to combat and overcome them.

If association with delusions could give you happiness, you should now have the best and most satisfactory form of happiness, because of your long association with delusions. But this is not the case. All of us are always under the sufferings of dissatisfaction and anxiety. The very start of our lives is marked with suffering, our lives end with suffering, and during our lives we go through all sorts of problems and miseries. Such is the nature of samsara, cyclic existence. The underlying cause of all this is that we are under the influence of contaminated body, actions, and delusions.

You should make it a point to free yourself from this yoke of delusions. Your feeling should have such urgency that you do not have time even to breathe before you mount your attack on them. When you only talk about the destructive nature of delusions, your attack on them is almost like mere backbiting, because it does not affect them directly.

First it is important to recognize the nature of the delusions and their destructive character, to discover what are the actual opponent forces that can counter them, and then to eliminate them. By applying the right opponent force you should be able to hit the target in the right way—that means employing the right opponent force to destroy the ignorance that is at the root of all the delusions. This ignorance refers to the misconception of reality that apprehends things as existing truly or inherently.

The root of all these sufferings is firmly based in the mind. As long as suffering is firmly based and has deep roots in you, any temporary relief that you may gain from the sufferings of lower existence is unstable and unreliable. The relief is like that of a criminal destined to be executed, who gains a temporary postponement of his execution—there is nothing much about which to be delighted.

Thus it is very important to reflect upon the suffering nature of life in this cycle of existence in general: the sufferings of uncertainty, the sufferings of lack of contentment, and the sufferings of having to discard the body again and again. If one were to make a pile of the heads of those whom one has killed in one's successive lives, it would far exceed the height of mountains. If one were to collect the drops of tears that one has shed for the loss of relatives and friends in the past, it would far exceed the vastness of oceans.

As the Buddha said in the sutras, in this cycle of existence which is like the tip of the needle there is no place for happiness. For instance, we Tibetans suffer on a national scale. In particular, the people inside Tibet live with great anxiety, while those who are scattered in other countries suffer the difficulties of migration. Suffering is present also for people living inside independent countries such as India: before they gained independence they had a lot of sufferings, and then even after independence has been attained they still have sufferings. In very powerful and developed countries such as the United States—although they are regarded as superpowers and are materially developed and superficially appear to be quite successful—at the level of the individual you find a lot of anxiety to the degree that many people have to live on sleeping pills and tranquilizers. When you reflect in such terms, you will find that right from birth we have many sufferings to which are added cultural pressures such as competitiveness and lack of contentment—if you have a thousand you need a hundred thousand, and if you have a hundred thousand you want a million dollars and so forth. There is always this suffering of want and lack of contentment. Suffering is limitless. Just as the Kadampa master Potawa said, "The never-ending chain of sufferings that we face in this cycle of existence is the true face of the cycle of existence."

In our lives there are many circumstances for suffering both from within our bodies and from external causes. Right at the time of birth, when our lives on this planet first begin, we create problems and sufferings, not only for ourselves, but also for our mothers. With great difficulty we are born; and even after birth, for months and years, we remain extremely fragile and vulnerable, always depending upon others' protection. We have to survive under all sorts of circumstances and hardships.

Our bodies, on their own, are composed of impure substances and therefore are nothing to be really attached to. Each of us regards our own body as most precious. Not only that, even others find it attractive. On this basis, many negative emotions arise within ourselves and others. Let us consider whether or not this body deserves to be so well preserved and examine its nature, its different components: skin, bones, blood, flesh, and so forth. As an example, let us take a piece of skin from a finger: when we take it off and keep it, after a while we find it very repulsive. The same would be true of our bones, marrow, blood; it is because of our misconceptions that we apprehend them as most precious and beautiful. We feel attached to our own body and attracted to others' bodies as well. So we live under illusions. If we probe deeper, we will never find, on the part of the body, anything that can be regarded as attractive. Compared to it, other living species, such as plants, flowers and so forth, look more clean. We find that the bodies of humans and animals are really very impure and unclean.

Now let us inquire as to the function of this body. If we consider the body on its own, we find that it appears almost as though its main task is to produce human waste. Daily we take food and then release it as waste; it is almost as though the purpose of taking food and nourishment is to produce these wastes. If we were to heap up all the flour, rice, and so forth that we might have consumed over the last several years, it will be really a very large quantity. Such reflection is quite frightening. It is as though we live in this world just to protect and preserve this composite of impure substances. So, the body *per se* is not precious.

Our consciousness resides within this body through a karmic force, and as our consciousness is karmically linked with such a body it is also under the influence of karmic contamination. Reflections upon the six and eight types of sufferings[28] mentioned in *Lamrim Chenmo* as the general aspects of cyclic existence are indeed very effective in generating a genuine aspiration to attain freedom from this unsatisfactory state of existence. We undergo our lives in this cycle of existence through such a process of suffering. Right now, due to the kindness of our previous lives we are not thrown into the abyss of the lower realms and as a result have obtained this human form. Now, the important point is to examine and judge whether or not there is a possibility of terminating this vicious cycle of birth and death. It is by the force of our attachment and attraction to objects that we spin around in the cycle of existence. Attachment is a negative state of mind induced by the misapprehension of the true mode of existence of phenomena. Such an ignorance is a distorted mind that misconceives the nature of phenomena. If we are able to see through the deception of this ignorance, we will be able to put an end to its arisal; thus the possibility of attaining liberation appears. This is because then only will we be able to put an end to our accumulation of negative karma and at the same time cease activating the imprints of past karma.

Judging by our own experiences in this life and those of others, it is very obvious that consciousness is a phenomenon susceptible to change and transformation. Due to the force of bad companionship and different conditions, people change for the worse, becoming very aggressive. Likewise we see human beings changing for the better, becoming more gentle, kind, and so forth. This is an indication that an impermanent phenomenon is changeable, and therefore is subject to transformation.

The effect of consciousness even upon the body is very obvious. There is no need for a spiritual teacher to point that out to us—even the doctors tell us to keep our minds calm and to be happy, and that because of our anxieties we suffer. Emotional disturbances result in physical illness.

There is no possibility that meditating on love and compassion could cause mental disturbances. Although it is possible that a feeling of unease could arise when one is meditating on strong compassion, this is very different from the mental disturbances that one has as a result of delusions. In his *Bodhisattvacaryavatara*, Shantideva says that generating a strong compassion can, in a way, increase one's anxiety, for one is concerned about not only one's own suffering but also that of others. However, I can say that there could never be a case of losing mental balance or having a nervous breakdown as a result of meditating on compassion.

On the other hand, there is definitely the possibility of having a nervous breakdown as a result of being under the strong influence of hatred, anger, desire and so forth. Since the very purpose of one's life is to live happily, it is important to recognize the negative states of mind and put an end to them and to identify the positive states of mind and try to enhance them. Doing this is a natural right that we all have; if we utilize that right, we stand to gain.

As I remarked earlier, delusion is a state of mind that is very obvious: when it arises within the mind, it causes mental disturbances and anxieties in the individual, and furthermore causes many problems and difficulties in society, often on a national scale. We find that, right from the beginning of human civilization, delusions are the real causes of problems, trouble, and conflict within society. It is delusion that forces one to be attracted and attached to one's own side and to feel hatred and anger toward the opposite side. With such an outlook, one creates the many divisions within the human community. All of these come about through the underlying force of the attachment to one's own self. When one totally disregards the happiness of others for the purpose of one's own happiness, all these conflicts, wars, and so forth come about.

The negative emotions such as hatred, anger and desire are the real enemies that disturb and destroy our mental happiness and cause disturbance in society. Therefore, they are to be totally abandoned; they do not have even the slightest potential for yielding happiness.

There are sometimes situations in which painful surgery is necessary to remove an unhealthy or diseased part of the body. Similarly, we should cut away the negative emotions and delusions. Suffering from these negative states is like suffering from a chronic disease: there is no possibility of happiness or healthiness as long as they remain.

If we are able to see the destructive nature of delusions we will naturally develop the deep conviction that as long as we are under their influence there is no possibility of happiness or peace. Right now, even while we are alive, we have all sorts of sufferings and anxieties and so forth. The contemplation on the sufferings that we have right now is enough—there is no need to contemplate the acute and intense sufferings of the lower realms. The question of whether or not it is possible to put an end to such sufferings becomes very important and relevant now.

Since it is the ignorance misapprehending the true nature of phenomena that is at the root of all the delusions, it is very important for us first of all to identify this ignorant mind. This should be done by first analyzing how things appear to us and how they actually exist. If the appearance that we have of phenomena is true and accords with their reality, then analytically seeking them should bring us closer to that of which we have the appearance, but this is not the case. When we analytically investigate, we find that there is a disparity between our perception and the way things exist.

When something appears to us as good, it appears to us as one hundred percent good, and when something appears to us as undesirable, it appears as though it were totally undesirable in its own right. As a result of such appearance we misapprehend the object, and then on this basis we misconceptualize its nature. At the moment that we have very strong anger towards an object, we experience the person toward whom we feel extremely angry as totally negative—right from the top of his crown to the bottom of his soles. When the force of the anger diminishes, then the person begins to appear to be a little better. A similar sequence of experiences is true in the case of desire. Aryadeva says in *Chatu-shataka Shastra* that when one is under a very strong influence of negative emotions, one is almost at the point of insanity. No sane person would like to be mad. If we live insanely, we stand to lose. When we lose our mental balance under the influence of negative emotions, we will not be able to work for our own benefit, let alone work for others'.

Although we have incarnated so many times within beginningless time, we have nothing substantially positive to show from having done so. If we continue in the present style, there will never be an end to the cycle of birth and death. There is not even a single person that we can totally rely upon in this cycle of existence, in the suffering of being subject to repeated fluctuations and having to undergo birth, sickness, old age and death again and again. When we take birth in the cycle of existence we do so alone; when we have to die at the end we also do so alone.

If there is a possibility of putting an end to this senseless cycle, then seeking the means of doing so is definitely a worthy venture for us. First, by employing the appropriate methods we should reduce the force of the delusions and then eventually get to their root and eliminate them. As I usually remark, I used to feel that if I ever gain a state of cessation, I shall really take a good rest. Once we have attained such a state, we could take a good rest and a real holiday, in the true sense of the word. Until we get to such a state, it is foolish for us to be complacent. When we have attained the state of cessation, we have truly reached a very secure ground.

We should reflect: "Why do I undergo this vicious cycle of life and death, tormented by all these sufferings? It is because of my not recognizing the delusions and eliminating them. At this point, when I have the opportunity to engage in the right practice due to the kindness of the spiritual master, may I generate genuine renunciation within my mind, and impelled by such renunciation may I be able to engage in the practices of the three trainings, thus leading myself to the attainment of liberation."

8 The Specific Sufferings of the Different Realms

The next practice is the contemplation on the sufferings specific to the various realms in this cycle of existence. Let us leave aside the question of sufferings in the lower realms, as even when one has taken rebirth as a human being, one undergoes eight types of suffering. Reflection on these is very important, because as human sufferings are something that one can recognize through experience, when one develops renunciation on their basis it is much stronger than if it were on the basis of a contemplation on other forms of sufferings that one cannot see at all. So one can develop deep renunciation on the basis of just the observable sufferings of human beings. These sufferings are very extensively explained in *Lamrim Chenmo*.

In the realm of demi-gods one is tormented by jealousy. Even for human beings, when they are under a strong influence of jealousy, such as that towards a neighbor, there is no room for happiness. The devas have the sufferings of combat with the demi-gods, and they also undergo acute sufferings when they are separated from the happy life of the deva realms. Although temporarily there are no obvious or manifest sufferings in the form and formless realms, since the beings there are under the influence of contaminated actions and delusions, the peaceful state enjoyed there is not permanent.

In short, your own contaminated aggregates, the body and mind, serve as the basis for the manifest sufferings of this life, and they also bring about the experiences of the suffering of sufferings and the changeable sufferings, not only in this lifetime but also in the future. Thus you should make the request to the spiritual master that you be totally free from the contaminated aggregates.

Having reflected on and contemplated the general and specific sufferings of cyclic existence, particularly emphasizing the sufferings of human beings which are very observable and also reflecting upon the destructive nature of the delusions, you will gradually see—due to the force of familiarity and meditation—all the worldly attractions as miserable and under the influence of contaminated actions and delusions. You will be able to see the pointlessness and futility of all worldly attractions. Let us make an analogy. When Tibetans visit Tibet under Chinese rule, even when they see new buildings such as hotels, schools, and so forth, they immediately think that these are nothing to be admired, in light of the whole country being under a repressive occupation. Similarly, you will have a conviction that worldly attractions will not be worth much due to their being under the domination of delusions and actions.

As a result of such a perception, you will get to a point where the wish to achieve liberation will come about spontaneously and naturally without any conscious effort on your part. This marks the point of having trained your mind in the stages of the path common to the middling scope. The criterion of having trained the mind in the stages of the path common to the practitioners of the small scope is being able to overcome attraction to the affairs of this lifetime and being able to develop concern for the affairs of one's future life. The criterion of having trained one's mind in the stages of the path common to the middling scope is generating an attitude spontaneously and naturally seeking to achieve liberation, through the force of seeing all cyclic existence in its suffering nature.

9 *The Path to Liberation*

On the path to liberation, you must reverse the cycle of existence. To do this, you must eliminate the delusions. Although there might be different views on the identity of ignorance due to differences in philosophical views of emptiness, if you are able to totally eliminate the subtle delusions—particularly the most subtle level of ignorance—by applying the appropriate opponent forces, then you will be able to free yourself from all the other delusions. But if you apply the opponent force only to the gross levels of the delusions, you will not be able to attain a permanent liberation. The recognition of the subtle delusions can be understood only on the basis of studying the writings of the highest Buddhist philosophical school, Madhyamika Prasangika.

Of all the delusions, the worst is the ignorance which misconceives the mode of being of phenomena. This incorrect apprehension of the true nature of existence is of two types, one focusing upon the person and one upon other phenomena. It misapprehends the object as existing inherently, independently, in its own right. The opponent force which dispels such ignorance is a wisdom that focuses upon that distorted view of the object and disproves the mode of apprehension of that distorted view. Without such an appropriate opponent force, you will not be able to root out that ignorance and directly eliminate it. Since it is the ignorance mistakenly apprehending inherent existence in all phenomena that serves as the root of all other delusions, you should generate the wisdom penetrating the real nature of phenomena, which correctly perceives things as lacking such true or inherent existence.

The opponent force powerful enough to eliminate the delusions should be a wisdom which combines calm abiding and special insight. In order to cultivate an advanced meditative stabilization that is free of both subtle mental sinking and mental excitement, first of all there should be a basis: the practice of morality, an abstaining from negative actions. Therefore, the path leading to liberation is comprised of the three higher trainings: the training of morality as the foundation, the training of meditative stabilization as the complementing factor, and the actual path which is the training of wisdom. By enhancing the practice of wisdom and by developing it to its fullest extent, you will be able to eliminate totally the delusions, particularly ignorance which misapprehends the mode of being of phenomena.

If the practitioner is motivated to achieve liberation for his own sake alone, he undertakes such a practice and gains the state free of delusions, the state of the arhat or "foe destroyer." But here we are engaged in the path that is common to the middling scope, with its ultimate aim of leading to the practices of a bodhisattva. Therefore, only one practice, the training in morality, is explained here, while the practices of the remaining two trainings, concentration and wisdom, are explained later.

The development of renunciation first is very important. Although the primary aim is to work for the benefit of others, in order to develop the compassion that is strong enough to feel the unbearableness of the sufferings of others, it is very important to have renunciation focusing initially upon your own sufferings, feeling them to be unbearable. Therefore, renunciation is a cause that will later lead to the generation of compassion.

Once your realization of renunciation has become powerful, the focus should be shifted from your own sufferings to those of others. Having identified the sufferings in yourself, you will be able to compare yourself with other sentient beings and think that all other sentient beings are equal to you in having the wish to free themselves from suffering and enjoy happiness.

In order to have a pure observance of morality, it is important to recognize the factors that do not accord with morality, such as the ten non-virtues and to abstain from them. Since ignorance is a door that leads to negative actions, it is very important to recognize the discordant factors to whatever vows you may have taken—lay or monastic. Without such knowledge, although you may feel that you have not transgressed any vows, because of your ignorance you are likely to break them. Therefore, ignorance must be overcome. In order to do this, first read and study the texts concerning the vows.

Being disrespectful is another door leading to negative actions. You should cultivate respect for the Buddha and the doctrine expounded by him, by reflecting on his kindness and great qualities. If you have deep respect towards the Buddha, you will be able to hold his doctrine and the vows more dear.

The lack of conscientiousness is also a door leading to negative actions and the transgression of vows, as is having an abundance of negative emotions. Although we must apply opponent forces to all the delusions, some of us have stronger specific emotions, such as desire or anger, than others. So you should give special attention to overcoming the strongest emotion by applying its specific antidote, such as meditation on love to counter anger, on ugliness to counter attachments, on breathing for anxiety, etc. Generally, you should seek conscientiousness, thinking, "I am a follower of the Buddha and I am a spiritual being." If you have such a faculty, you will be able to restrain and protect yourself from negative actions, even in dreams. That is how you should observe pure morality.

Any path that enables you to purify your mind from negativities is a path leading to liberation. You should not have the notion that liberation is a place far away; rather, the cessation of ignorance within your mind is liberation. It is called liberation because it is a freedom from the bondage of the sufferings and delusions. Although such a state of liberation is a very high condition, its attainment does not mark the total fulfillment of one's aspirations. For although at that point one has attained permanent peace, freed oneself from cyclic existence, and eliminated delusions, one is not yet free from the subtle influences and the residual imprints implanted in one's psyche by these delusions. These latent imprints still distort the appearance of phenomena and cause a dualistic view, thus obstructing the attainment of omniscience. Therefore, in terms of realization, the state of the arhat—that of personal liberation—is not final.

10 The Mind of Great Capacity

From one point of view, personal liberation without freeing others is selfish and unfair, because all sentient beings also have the natural right and desire to be free of suffering. Therefore, it is important for practitioners to engage in the practice of the stages of the path of the highest scope, starting with the generation of bodhicitta. Bodhicitta, the altruistic aspiration to achieve enlightenment for the benefit of all sentient beings, is the factor that determines whether or not one is a Mahayanist. Therefore, bodhicitta is the sole gateway to the Mahayana path. The moment the faculty of bodhicitta becomes degenerated, one is no longer a bodhisattva. Once one has cultivated bodhicitta, all the meritorious actions that are supported by and complemented with this altruism—even the slightest form of positive action—become causes for the achievement of omniscience.

Omniscience is a wisdom that is able to perceive directly all phenomena, both the ultimate and the conventional natures, simultaneously. It is a state where all the potentials of one's wisdom are developed fully and where there is also a total freedom from all the obstructions to knowledge. It can be achieved only by purifying all the faults of one's mind, and only by complementing the practice of wisdom with the practices of method: bodhicitta, compassion, and so forth.

Without this factor of method, bodhicitta, even though one might have great wisdom—the wisdom realizing emptiness such as that of the *sravakas* and *pratyekabuddhas*—one will not be able to achieve the omniscient state. It is said that the direct realization of emptiness by the bodhisattvas on the first level, which corresponds to the third of the five paths, the path of seeing, is able to surpass the realization of even the arhats.

When engaging in the meditation of generating bodhicitta, if you visualize your root guru in the aspect of and inseparable from Avalokiteshvara, the bodhisattva of compassion, your practice will gain great inspiration. Doing this will enable you to receive powerful inspirations to overcome all manifestations of self-cherishing thoughts within yourself. Therefore, as the preliminary to your meditation on bodhicitta, visualize your root guru as Avalokiteshvara and make fervent requests to him that you may be able to root out the self-centered attitudes from your mind.

In order to cultivate a genuine bodhicitta, you have to depend upon the proper methods and the instructions outlining these. There are two major systems of instructions, one the seven-point cause and effect method, the other the equalizing and exchanging oneself with others. These methods are equally efficacious in enabling a person to generate bodhicitta, but the latter is more profound and is also more effective. From one point of view, the latter method is designed for beings of higher faculty. So the different methods will suit the various mental dispositions of the different practitioners; some might find one more effective than the other. The tradition is that these methods are combined and practiced together.

11   The Seven-Point Cause and Effect Method

THE PRELIMINARY STEP OF CULTIVATING EQUANIMITY

The foundation for practicing the seven-point cause and effect method is cultivating a mind of equanimity. Without this foundation you will not be able to have an impartial altruistic view, because without equanimity you will always have partiality towards your relatives and friends. Realize that you should not have prejudice, hatred, or desire towards enemies, friends, or neutral persons, and thus lay a very firm foundation of equanimity.

To do this, as this text recommends, first visualize a neutral person whom you do not know at all. When you clearly visualize that person, you will find that you don't feel any fluctuations of emotion, no desire or hatred—you are indifferent. Then visualize an enemy; when you visualize the enemy clearly you will have a natural reaction of hatred, feeling all sorts of ill will. Next, clearly visualize a friend or relative to whom you feel very close. With that visualization, the natural reaction will be a feeling of affection and attachment.

With the visualization of your enemy, you will feel somewhat distant and will have hatred and a sense of repulsion. Consider enemies such as the Chinese, who meted out destruction on the dharma, who did not have compassion and only harmed other fellow human beings, who rule a country only through totalitarian methods by snatching away the basic human qualities of trust and confidence. Reflect upon your justification in reacting so negatively to them. Although it is true that they have meted out much harm and destruction in this life, have they always done such things and been like this? You will find that they have not: in the past they must have engaged in actions beneficial to you and many others. But right now they have no faith in the dharma and have meted out harm and destruction to many people. They have almost no control over themselves. Because of being under the influence of ignorance, hatred, and so forth, they have these faults; it is not their essential nature.

Reflect that delusions are within your own mind also. Although there might be a difference in the force of these delusions, in terms of being delusions they are delusions equally. You should decide that there is not much point in emotionally reacting to the people you have categorized as enemies.

Then examine how you react, on the other hand, to your relatives and friends. You might think that they have been very kind to you, they have benefited you in such and such a way, and so forth. You might also have the feeling, with those who are very close, that you would even be prepared to sacrifice your life for them. Although it is true that they have been kind to you in this life, in the past they might have been your enemies, and even gone to the extent of taking your life. They might have meted out harm and destruction to many other living beings. Therefore, there is no point in being absolutely or permanently attached to such people, categorizing them as your friends and relatives.

Thus, there is not much difference between enemies and friends as far as yourself is concerned. They have both had times of benefiting you and they have both had times of harming you. Your having partiality towards them is groundless.

Therefore, develop the mind of equanimity directed towards all sentient beings. This mind cannot be brought about by meditating just once or twice, but rather through repeated meditations over months or years.

1   RECOGNIZING SENTIENT BEINGS AS HAVING BEEN ONE'S MOTHER

The first step of the seven-point cause and effect method is to cultivate the recognition of all sentient beings as having been one's mother. To do this, it is first necessary to reflect on your beginningless lives in this cycle of existence and that through many of your lives you have had to depend on your mothers. There is not a single living being that you can definitely point to as not having been your mother in the past. Perceive all sentient beings as having been your own kind mothers. You might wonder how, since sentient beings are infinite and numberless, you can say that all of them have been your mother. But consider that just as sentient beings are numberless, your lives in this cycle of existence have been numberless as well. You might also reflect that although other sentient beings have been your mothers, they have been so in the past and not in this life. But what about your mother of yesterday, is she not still your mother?

If you are able to understand the beginninglessness of your lives, you will be able to understand that you have taken many forms of life—such as egg born and womb born—that require a mother. You will find that there is not a single sentient being that has not been your mother in the past. Realization of this is quite difficult. You could start with the opposite approach—the exclusion of those that might never have been your mother. That is, you could think that it is possible that some sentient beings have not been your mother; but then, whom could you point out, with complete assurance, as not once having been your mother?

Next, examine whether you stand to gain or lose by cultivating this recognition of others as mothers. Since you are concerned with cultivating bodhicitta, the altruistic aspiration, you should recognize that if you do not have this basic factor of recognition of others as having been your mothers, you will not have success in its cultivation. So, by not developing this recognition you stand to lose. If by disbelieving that all sentient beings have been your mothers, you stood to gain, that would be fine, but this is not the case. Because of the beginninglessness of your lives in this cycle of existence, all sentient beings have been your mothers.

A recognition of others as being your dearest ones need not be confined to recognizing them as mothers alone. As Maitreya recommends in his *Abhisamayalankara*, you can also view them as having been your best friends or closest relatives. For example, you can view all sentient beings as having been your fathers, if you relate better to your father than to your mother, or as children to whom you feel closest and for whom you have the deepest affection. The point is to bring about an effect within your mind and to develop a state of mind that will enable you to perceive all living beings as the closest objects of affection and kindness. That is how you cultivate the recognition of sentient beings as having been one's mother.

Some arguments have been raised in the text, such as if sentient beings have been your mothers, surely you should be able to recall this fact. The text replies that such a lack of remembrance does not constitute proof, because even in this life some children do not recognize their mothers due to the passage of time. So, just as your mother of this life is very kind and is an object of love and affection, all sentient beings should equally be objects of love and affection.

2 RECOLLECTION OF ALL BEINGS' KINDNESS

The next meditation is on the recollection of the kindness of all beings. For this, you should visualize the person to whom you feel closest—be it your mother or father—when she or he is quite old. Clearly visualize the person at an age when she or he depends upon others' cooperation and assistance. Do-

ing this has a special significance, for it will make your meditation more powerful and effective.

Then think that your mother, for example, has been your
mother not only in this lifetime, but also in past lives. Particularly in this life her kindness was boundless at the time of
your birth, and before that during gestation she had to undergo all sorts of hardships, and even after birth her affection
was such that she was able to surrender her own happiness
and pleasure for the sake of the happiness and pleasure of her
child. At the time of your birth she felt as joyful as if she had
found a treasure, and according to her own capacities she has
protected you, cleaning even your filth. You were thus protected until you could stand on your own feet.

This kindness is also experienced when you take rebirth as
animals, such as birds, dogs, and kittens. You can observe
them: Although these animals' affection is not as enduring
as that of humans, at the time of birth, the mothers have very
strong love and affection. From one point of view, their affection and compassion to their small ones are much more self-
less, since the affection and compassion of human beings are
slightly influenced by the selfishness of thinking that the children will later serve and return affection. This is not the case
with animals.

Birds, for example, even feed their small ones by killing insects and so forth. Certain types of birds, when they protect
their babies, sacrifice a great deal and they do it individually,
not living in communities as do human beings. The manner
in which they bring up their small ones is really very touching. When their young are threatened by danger such as that
from cats or vultures, they even sacrifice their lives if they must.
Basically, they do so out of attachment, but still their act is
a great kindness—so it is not only when you take rebirth as
a human being that the kindness of mothers is boundless. Their
kindness is not confined to one life alone but to many lifetimes. This kind of contemplation will have a very strong effect within your mind.

After reflecting upon the kindness of mothers, particularly

of this lifetime, you should visualize other beings whom you find quite distant and repulsive, even animals, and take them as your object of visualization. Think that although these enemies are harmful to you and are your adversaries in this life, in past lives they must have been your most dear parents and must have even protected and saved your life countless times. Therefore, their kindness is boundless. In such a manner you should train your mind.

3 REPAYING KINDNESS

The meditation on the recollection of kindness should be followed by meditation upon repaying that kindness. The thought to repay the kindness of mothers will come about naturally when you have been successful in recollecting this kindness—it should come from the depths of your heart. Not to repay their kindness would be unfair and ungrateful of you. Therefore, you should work according to your own capacity for the benefit of others; doing this repays their kindness.

4 LOVING KINDNESS

Having cultivated equanimity and the recognition of all sentient beings as having been one's mother, you will see all sentient beings as objects of affection and endearment. And the more forceful your feeling of affection towards them, the stronger will be your aspiration that they be free from suffering and enjoy happiness. So the recognition of others as having been one's mother is the foundation for the subsequent meditations. Having laid that proper foundation, recollected their kindness, and developed the genuine wish to repay it, you gain a state wherein you feel close to and affectionate towards all living beings. Now reflect that all these sentient beings, although they naturally desire happiness and wish to avoid suffering, are tormented by unimaginable sufferings. Reflect upon the fact that they are just like yourself in desiring hap-

piness, but they lack this happiness. By such reflection cultivate loving kindness.

5   GREAT COMPASSION

When you do the meditation on compassion, reflect upon the
manner in which sentient beings undergo the experience of
suffering. First, in order to have a very strong force of compassion, visualize a being undergoing active sufferings. For example, as the text here recommends, you could vividly and
clearly visualize an animal destined to be killed by a butcher.
Imagine in what kind of mental state such a being would be
when facing such a situation. Then develop the strong wish
that this particular being be free of that suffering.

You could also visualize the sufferings of other living beings. For example, when one travels in India by train, one sees
many suffering creatures at the railway stations—dogs and other
animals, and even human beings. Imagine these creatures and
think that they are all equal to yourself in having the natural
wish to have happiness and avoid suffering, yet nevertheless
they undergo very obvious and manifest sufferings. Human
beings employ animals for all sorts of purposes, and they are
put to very hard, laborious work. One sees many oxen in the
towns and villages; although Indian society prevents the killing of these animals and therefore they do not face immediate
extinction, when they are grown up and their use to the community is over, they are neglected. In India, one also sees
beggars—blind, deaf, dumb, paralysed and so on—and very
poor people. Instead of helping them with compassion, people tend to either avoid or intimidate them, even going so far
as to hit them. One can see all these things at any railway
station.

You can visualize any situation that you find unbearable. Doing so will enable you to have a strong force of compassion
and make it easier to develop a genuine universal compassion.

Then think about the sentient beings in other categories;
they may not be undergoing manifest sufferings right now, but

due to indulging in negative actions that will definitely produce undesirable consequences in the future, they are certain to face such experiences, too.

The wish that all sentient beings who lack happiness be endowed with happiness is the state of mind called universal love, and the wish that sentient beings be free of suffering is called compassion. These two meditations can be undertaken in combination, until there is some kind of effect or change in your mind.

6 THE UNUSUAL ATTITUDE

Your cultivation of love and great compassion should not be left in a state of mere imagination or wish alone; rather, a sense of responsibility, a genuine intention to engage in the task of relieving sentient beings of their sufferings and providing them with happiness, should be developed. It is important for a practitioner to work for and take upon himself or herself the responsibility of fulfilling this intention. The stronger your cultivation of compassion is, the more committed you will feel to taking this responsibility. Because of their ignorance, sentient beings do not know the right methods by which they can fulfill their aims. It is the responsibility of those who are equipped with this knowledge to fulfill the intention of working for their benefit.

Such a state of mind is called the extraordinary attitude or special, unusual attitude. It is called unusual or extraordinary because such a force of compassion, committing oneself to taking on such a responsibility, is not to be found in the trainees of lower capacity. As the oral traditions explain, with this extraordinary attitude there is a commitment that one will take upon oneself the responsibility of fulfilling this aim. It is like striking a deal in business and signing a contract.

After generating the extraordinary attitude, ask yourself whether or not, although you have developed the strong courage and the determination to work for the benefit of other sentient beings, you really possess the capacity and capability to bring them genuine happiness. It is only by your showing living beings the right path leading towards omniscience, and by living beings on their part eliminating the ignorance within themselves, that they will be able to gain lasting happiness. Although you may be able to work for other sentient beings to bring them temporary happiness, bringing about their ultimate aims is possible only when these beings take upon themselves the initiative to eliminate the ignorance within themselves. The same is true of yourself: If you desire the attainment of liberation, it is your responsibility to take the initiative to eliminate the ignorance within yourself.

As I just mentioned, you must also show the right path to living beings—and for that, first of all, you must possess the knowledge yourself. There are different ways of possessing knowledge; one is by developing an intellectual understanding, but the more profound way is understanding through experience.

The teaching that you are going to give to others should not be obscure to yourself. You should also have the perfect wisdom that can judge the suitability and appropriateness of a teaching for the dispositions and mental faculties of different beings. Because some things are profound, you cannot teach them to just anyone; some teachings might prove more harmful than beneficial to some types of people.

To possess a knowledge of the different faculties of all beings, you will have to overcome all subtle forms of obstructions to knowledge. An example given by the Buddha himself during his life demonstrates this importance: A householder wanted to become a monk, but Buddha's disciples of high caliber such as Sariputra did not see that the person had sufficient virtuous potential within his mind to be eligible to take ordination. But the Buddha, through the force of his omniscience, saw such a seed within him. Therefore, so long as you yourself are not completely enlightened there will always be an inner obstruction to knowledge that will make your task of helping others incomplete.

You might feel that since fulfilling the wishes of other sentient beings and bringing about their welfare basically depends upon them taking the initiative themselves, then what particular need is there for you to work for the achievement of enlightenment? After all, there are many buddhas who will be able to help the sentient beings immediately if these beings take the initiative.

However, the benefit from particular spiritual guides or teachers depends upon the recipient having karmic links with these beings. Thus, some spiritual teachers can be most effective and beneficial to only a certain number of disciples, and not to other beings. In order to understand this, it is helpful to read the sutras, such as *The Perfection of Wisdom in Eight Thousand Lines*, in which the buddhas and bodhisattvas, having seen that a certain practitioner had a stronger karmic link with another spiritual teacher, advised him to seek his own spiritual master. There will be sentient beings who may be able to see a buddha directly, but who may not benefit as much from that as they would from interaction with you, due to their having a deeper karmic link with you. Since life is beginningless in this cycle of existence, one can speak of beginningless karmic links; however, what I am concerned with and referring to here is a strong karmic link between individuals formed in recent lives.

Although your achievement of the omniscient state may not be beneficial to all living beings, it will definitely bring a lot of practical benefit to certain living beings. Therefore, it is very important that you work for your own achievement of the completely enlightened state. Because there might be living beings who depend very much upon your guidance on the spiritual path, it is important that you take upon yourself the responsibility to work for the benefit of others. By thinking in such terms, you will be able to develop the strong belief that without attaining the omniscient state you will not be able to fulfill what you set out to do and truly benefit others.

7   BODHICITTA

Based on the foundation of love and compassion, you should generate from the depths of your heart the aspiration to achieve the completely enlightened state for the benefit of all sentient beings. The cultivation of such a mind constitutes the realization of bodhicitta.

After the meditation on generating bodhicitta you should engage in the practice of cultivating bodhicitta that takes the result into the path. Visualizing the spiritual guru at your crown, imagine that the guru expresses delight, saying that it is very admirable and you are very fortunate that you have generated bodhicitta and have engaged in the path of cultivating it, and that he shall take you under his care. Imagine that, as a result of the guru's delight, he dissolves through your crown and into your heart. Then you dissolve into emptiness and from emptiness arise in the aspect of Buddha Shakyamuni. See yourself becoming inseparable from him, and rejoice. At your heart visualize all your virtues accumulated through the practice of bodhicitta. These emanate, in the form of light rays, toward all living beings and actively work for their benefit, relieving them of their suffering, placing them in the state of liberation and favorable rebirth, and eventually leading them to the omniscient state.

During the between-session periods, you should read texts that are related to the practice of bodhicitta. With that the method of cultivating bodhicitta according to the seven-point cause and effect method is concluded.

12 Equalizing and Exchanging Oneself with Others

Next follows the instruction on the cultivation of bodhicitta according to the method of equalizing and exchanging oneself with others. This meditation has five sections: (1) equalizing oneself with others; (2) reflecting on the disadvantages of the self-cherishing attitude from many perspectives; (3) reflecting on the advantages of the thought cherishing the welfare of others from many perspectives; (4) the actual exchange of oneself and others; and (5) taking and giving.

1 EQUALIZING ONESELF WITH OTHERS

This phrase refers to the practice of reflecting upon the equality of oneself and others in having the natural and spontaneous wish to enjoy happiness and avoid suffering. For the generation of this type of equanimity, the instruction by the late Kyabje Trijang Rinpoche on the nine-round meditation is very powerful and effective.

Meditation on Equanimity

The nine-round meditation is comprised of training the mind in equanimity with a mental outlook based on the dual nature of things and events: the conventional and the ultimate. Based on different perspectives, the first in turn is divided into two sections, one from the viewpoint of others and the second from the viewpoint of oneself.

The rounds of visualization on cultivating equanimity from the viewpoint of others are divided into three:

a) Develop the thought that all sentient beings are equal insofar as the natural wish to avoid suffering is concerned and that therefore there is no point in being partial or discriminatory.

b) Reflect that all sentient beings equally desire happiness and therefore there is no ground for discriminating between them when working for their benefit. The situation is analogous to one where you encounter ten equally wretched beggars who are desperately asking you to relieve their hunger. In such circumstances it is senseless to have any feeling of preference.

c) Develop an equanimity based on the reflection that all sentient beings are equal in lacking genuine happiness although they have the innate desire to possess it. Likewise all sentient beings are the same in having suffering and the wish to avoid it. If there are ten patients equally suffering a serious illness, there is no justification for a doctor to discriminate when treating them. Similarly, there is no moral justification for you to be biased when helping others to relieve their sufferings.

With the above three types of practice you train your mind in the attitude expressed as follows: "I shall never discriminate between beings and will always work equally to help them overcome suffering and gain happiness."

The next three rounds of meditation enforce the thought that there is no justification for discrimination between sentient beings from the point of view of oneself or from the viewpoint of others. This training is divided into three sections:

a) You might have the thought that although reflection upon the equality of others is fairly persuasive regarding the futility of your being discriminatory towards other beings, surely when viewed from your own side the situation will look quite different. After all, some people are friends and help you, whereas many others harm you. To counter this thought which attempts to give false grounds for being partial towards others, reflect that all sentient beings are equally kind to you: They have all been at one time or other your closest friends and relatives. Hence there is no rational basis at all for being biased towards or against any.

b) Perhaps you have the idea that although people have been your friends in the past, they have equally been your enemies and have caused harm as well. Such notions should be countered by reflecting that sentient beings' kindness to you is not confined to when they are friends and relatives alone; their kindness when they are your enemies is boundless. The enemy provides you with the precious opportunity to train yourself in the noble ideals of patience and tolerance, traits vital for the perfection of your generation of universal compassion and bodhicitta. For a bodhisattva who emphasizes the practice of bodhicitta, the training in patience is indispensable. Contemplating upon such lines of reasoning will persuade you that there are no grounds for neglecting the welfare of even a single sentient being.

c) Reflect that, as Shantideva wrote in *Bodhisattvacaryavatara*, there is no sense in someone who is himself subject to suffering and impermanence being selfish and discriminatory towards others who are also tormented by the same fate. For example, it would be quite senseless and stupid for ten convicted criminals who are sentenced for execution within a short time by the law to argue between themselves, for their days are numbered.

The next three rounds of meditation deal with the cultivation of equanimity based on an insight into the ultimate nature of things and events. (This "ultimate" should not be taken to refer to the ultimate truth in terms of emptiness—rather, it means that the outlook adopted in these visualizations is deeper and hence relatively ultimate in comparison to the earlier meditations.)

a) Consider whether or not there are any "true" enemies

in the real sense of the word. If there are, then the fully enlightened buddhas should perceive them as such, which is
definitely not the case. For a buddha, all sentient beings are
equally dear. Also, when you examine deeply, you will find
that it is in fact the delusions within the enemies and not the
enemies themselves that actually cause harm. Aryadeva said
in his *Chatu-shataka Shastra*:

> Buddhas see the delusion as the enemy
> And not the childish who possess it.

Therefore, there is no justification at all for you to hold grudges
against those who cause harm, and neglect the welfare of such
beings.

b) Secondly, ask yourself whether these so-called enemies
are permanent and will always remain as enemies or whether
they are changeable. Concluding that they are not permanent
will enable you to overcome your disinterest in their welfare.

c) The last meditation is a reflection upon the relative nature of "enemy" and "friend," and touches upon the ultimate nature of phenomena. Concepts of enemy, friend and
so forth are relative and exist only at the conventional level.
They are mutually dependent, as are the concepts of long and
short. A person may be an enemy in relation to one person
while at the same time being a dear friend to another. It is
your misapprehension of friends, relatives and enemies as inherently existent that gives rise to your fluctuating emotions
towards them. Therefore, by realizing that there is no such
inherently existent enemy and friend, you will be able to overcome your biased feelings towards all beings.

These techniques are all very effective for transforming the
mind. In employing such methods of visualization you should
cultivate equanimity. In short, meditate on this theme as
summed up in a verse in the *Lama Choepa* guru yoga:

> As no one desires even the slightest suffering
> Nor ever has enough of happiness,
> There is no difference between myself and others;
> Therefore, inspire me to rejoice when others are happy.

The instruction for training one's mind in the method of equalizing and exchanging oneself with others is best found in *Bodhisattvacaryavatara*. This text—particularly the sixth chapter, the chapter on patience—is in fact like a king among all the texts dealing with the thought transformation practices.

When you are able to perceive enemies as kind to you, you will have overcome a great stumbling block, because the enemy is the greatest stumbling block for the cultivation of the thought cherishing the welfare of others. From this viewpoint, the very factor that normally serves as an obstacle and stumbling block for others in their spiritual progress is transformed into a favorable condition and actually becomes an impetus for practice. This mindset is indeed effective and powerful. The instruction for the cultivation of this mind of equality, explained in the eighth chapter of *Bodhisattvacaryavatara*, the chapter on concentration, is to be practiced in particular.

2 REFLECTION ON THE DISADVANTAGES OF THE SELF-CHERISHING ATTITUDE

The next step is the contemplation—from many different perspectives—upon the disadvantages and faults of the self-cherishing attitude. As Geshe Chekawa said in his *Lojong dhon dun ma* (Seven Points on Thought Transformation)[29]: "Banish the one object of all blame." It is the self-cherishing attitude that is the source of all miseries and therefore is the only object to be blamed for all misfortune. Normally, because of our self-righteousness, it is quite natural for us to blame others when something happens that we do not like, such as problems, suffering, and so forth. We immediately blame it upon others, but if we think in real terms we will find that all the problems and undesirable experiences come about because of the kind of body that we have assumed, the body that is contaminated and a product of actions and delusions. We possess such a body because of our attachment to our self; therefore, it is attachment and grasping at the self that give rise to all these undesirable sufferings.

Since the self-cherishing and self-grasping attitudes abide strongly fortified within our minds, we have never been able to shake them in the least. We have so far not been able to disturb them even as much as a small pebble in a shoe would disturb a person.

If we remain with our present outlook and way of thinking, we will still be under the influence and command of these two factors. We should reflect that these factors have always caused our downfall in the past, and that they will do so in the future if we remain under their influence.

In deeper terms, we will find that all the sufferings and problems and anxieties of not finding what we seek, of being separated from our loved ones, of physical illnesses, of suffering from want, lack of contentment, quarrels and so forth, come about because of our underlying attachment to the self and the self-cherishing attitude that tries to protect such a self within ourselves. The more selfish a person is, the more sufferings and anxieties he or she will have. This self-cherishing attitude manifests in all sorts of ways, which results in problems and anxieties. Yet we never recognize the truth—that these are all the doings of the self-cherishing attitude. Rather, we have the tendency to blame others and external factors: "He did it, and if he had done something else, it wouldn't have happened."

Even on a global level, if we search for the real cause of the two world wars and all the violence that fills human history, we will find that they all eventually trace back to the self-cherishing and self-grasping attitudes. The same is true of all the problems and conflicts within our world during the present age.

Even the problems we find at the family level and national level are due to the self-cherishing attitude and selfish thoughts. For example, in an argument between two people, each side will truly feel that it has more truth than the other; so if one side cannot submit and admit fault, then a physical fight may eventually ensue. When we have arguments, if one of the parties accepts the disputed matter as its own fault, then the argument will deflate right there, just like a punctured tire. We find that all these problems come about due to selfish thought, the thought that we did what was right but the others did not act correctly. The following verse from *Lama Choepa* sums this up quite succinctly:

> This chronic disease of cherishing myself
> Is the cause of unwanted suffering;
> Perceiving this, may I be inspired
> To blame, begrudge and destroy
> This self-cherishing demon.

3 REFLECTION ON THE ADVANTAGES OF THE THOUGHT CHERISHING THE WELFARE OF OTHERS

Having realized the enormous disadvantages of holding on to a selfish thought cherishing your welfare alone, you should now reflect upon the kindness of all mother sentient beings, as discussed earlier. The kindness of other beings towards us is boundless while we revolve in this cycle of existence. This is particularly true when we first embark upon a spiritual path and thus begin the process of untying the chains that bind us to this cyclic existence. Let us take the example of our present life and its survival in the human community. In this age, economic development is believed to be one of the most vital factors contributing to the happiness of a community, and it can be achieved only through the cooperation of others. Although two nations may have differences on many political issues, when they realize the importance of having economic links they will cooperate so as to achieve mutual economic benefit.

Even people who are totally anti-religious will accept and admit that the welfare of the masses is more important than the welfare of an individual. If the community is successful, then the individual will derive benefit from it: on the other hand, if one or two individuals are successful, but the community is failing, then sooner or later the individuals living in the community will face the consequences of such a failure. Therefore, when we work for the benefit of the masses, the fulfillment of our personal aims comes as a by-product. But if we are concerned with our own selfish aims, we will not achieve them. This is not merely a religious matter; it is a fact we can observe even in the worldly arena.

We find that if a person lives a very selfish life and is never concerned about the welfare of others, he will have few friends, and people will not take much notice of him. At the time of his death, there will not be many people who will regret his passing. Some deceptive and negative persons may be very powerful and wealthy, and therefore some people—for economic reasons and so forth—might portray themselves as friends, but they will speak against such persons behind their backs. When these negative persons die, these very same "friends" may rejoice at their death.

On the other hand, many people mourn and regret the death of a person who is very kind and always altruistic and who works for the benefit of others. We find that altruism, as well as the person who possesses it, is regarded as the friend of all, and it becomes the object of veneration and respect by others.

I often remark, partly in jest, that if one really wants to be selfish, one should be "wisely selfish" by working for others. By helping others, one will receive help and assistance in return, particularly when one is in a hard situation—the time when one needs assistance from others the most. But if one tries to be very selfish, then when one is in difficult circumstances, one will find fewer people who are willing to help and one will be left to resolve the situation and difficulty on one's own. It is the nature of human beings to depend upon the cooperation and assistance of others, particularly when facing difficult times; during such times and during hardship it is only true friends who will be beneficial and helpful. By living an unselfish life, one will be able to earn genuine friends, whereas selfish thoughts and a selfish life will never gain one genuine and true friends.

The essence of Mahayana practice is really to teach us the methods by which we will be able to succeed not only in this life but also in the future. Such instruction is, in fact, very practical and relevant to all—believers and non-believers alike. If we are able to derive practical benefits within this lifetime by living a virtuous life, we will be able to fulfill the wishes of future lifetimes as well.

As the great bodhisattva Shantideva said in his *Bodhisatt-vacaryavatara*, there is no need to talk at great length about the advantages of the thought cherishing the welfare of others and the disadvantages and faults of the self-cherishing attitude. We need only compare ourselves, who are under the grip of the self-cherishing attitude, and the buddhas, who have abandoned such an attitude and who always cherish others, in order to see the disadvantages and advantages of the two types of mind.

The meaning of the assertion that the Buddha is very precious and exceptional should not be confined to the Buddha's having major and minor noble marks alone; rather, the words point to the Buddha's being always under the strong influence of compassion to its fullest extent. Since compassion is a true source of benefit and happiness, a being who has developed it to the fullest extent is someone whom we can truly admire and respect.

The *Bodhisattvacaryavatara* states:

> If I do not exchange my happiness
> For the sufferings of others,
> I shall not attain the state of Buddhahood
> And even in cyclic existence shall have no joy.

In the same vein, *Lama Choepa* reads:

> Cherishing myself is the gateway to all failures,
> While cherishing my mothers is the basis of all success.
> Inspire me to make the core of my practice
> The yoga of exchanging myself for others.

The original idea or motive of Karl Marx—founder of the philosophy that is the basis of the Chinese system—was to a large extent positive: it was to work for the benefit of the masses. Where it went wrong was that its actual practice was moved by resentment and confrontation based on a class struggle. The revolutionaries did not emphasize and enhance the practice of altruism. Because their approach was based on confrontation, with hatred between classes, they ended up having many poor in their society, rather than fulfilling what they originally had set out to achieve. This is a very good example of how hatred breeds suffering.

Buddhist writings emphasize the practice of overcoming selfish attitudes and generating the wish cherishing the welfare of others, which really is the true source of happiness and should be practiced by socialist countries to fulfill their aims. Reflecting upon the disadvantages of the self-cherishing thought and the advantages of the thoughts cherishing the benefit of others is in fact the true essence of the teachings on thought transformation. Having been convinced of this, one should undertake the practice of exchanging oneself with others.

4   THE ACTUAL EXCHANGE OF ONESELF WITH OTHERS

To exchange oneself with others is to reverse a former attitude: The thought of endearment and cherishing of oneself with its feeling of indifference towards others should now be reversed as follows. One should feel indifferent to oneself, reduce the force of clinging to oneself, and rather hold the welfare of other sentient beings as precious. That is the meaning of exchanging oneself with others. The degree of high value one feels towards oneself should now be turned towards others.

For this practice, one should also be knowledgeable about the commitments and precepts[30] of thought transformation practices. If one undertakes such a practice one will be able to transform any adverse circumstances into favorable conditions of the path. In this age of degeneration when one meets with all sorts of problems and adverse circumstances, the practice of thought transformation is very effective. If someone lacks the practice of thought transformation, even though that person might be a very serious meditator he or she will meet with many hardships and hurdles.

5 GIVING AND TAKING

The practice of the actual exchange of oneself with others should be followed by the practice of giving and taking. The latter is begun by reflecting that although all mother sentient beings desire happiness, they lack it, and that although they do not desire suffering, they undergo it. Think that it is the ignorance of sentient beings that impels them to work for the fulfillment of their selfish aims.

You should develop the unusual, extraordinary attitude of wishing that all their sufferings ripen upon yourself. This meditation on taking and giving is quite powerfully presented in *Lama Choepa*[31] in the following verse:

> Therefore, O venerable compassionate gurus,
> Inspire me that all karmic obscurations and sufferings
>   of mother sentient beings
> Ripen upon me right now,
> And may I give others my happiness and merits
> In order that all beings enjoy happiness.

And the great master Nagarjuna said in his *Ratnavali*:

> May their negative fruits ripen upon me
> And my positive fruits upon them.

Induced by the strong sense of compassion for other sentient beings, visualize taking all their sufferings upon yourself; and then, induced by the strong wish of love, visualize giving away from the depths of your heart all your virtuous collections, happiness, wealth, possessions, even your body, to other sentient beings.

Make the wish that through the force of your virtuous collections all sentient beings may experience their desirable consequences: May those who wish a favorable rebirth attain it, and may those who wish material possessions obtain them. Imagine that your virtues are transformed into the objects desired by all these sentient beings and that all sentient beings obtain them.

The practice of giving can be undertaken even in regards to your own spiritual gurus: you can give your virtuous collection to your guru so that the guru lives a long time in order to work longer for the benefit of other sentient beings. On the other hand, the practice of taking can be done only in regards to sentient beings, those who have not attained the highest form of enlightenment. From the bodhisattvas on the highest level you should imagine taking upon yourself the obstructions to knowledge that they have within themselves.

When you engage in the practice of taking, just as both *Bodhisattvacaryavatara* and the thought transformation text explain, you should first try to train yourself by imagining taking your own future sufferings upon yourself right now. Then, once you gain practice, apply the process to the sufferings of others.

Chekawa writes in his *Lojong dhon dun ma* (Seven Points on Thought Transformation):

> Practice in combination
> Both giving and taking.
> Commence the taking from your side.
> Place these two astride the breath.

If you can conjoin such practices with the breathing process—that is, imagining taking when inhaling and giving when exhaling—you will be able to engage in a powerful practice, leading you to the strong commitment that you will engage in the bodhisattva deeds. If you are able to engage in such a powerful practice, then due to the strong determination and commitment that you make as a result of cultivating bodhicitta, you will be able to alleviate the forces of the powerful and vast stores of negative actions committed in past lives, and also accumulate great stores of merit.

That is how you should train your mind in the cultivation of bodhicitta through the method of equalizing and exchanging yourself and others. When you are engaged in such a comprehensive practice, whether or not all sentient beings have been one's mother does not make much difference. The fact that every sentient being has the natural tendency to desire happiness and shun suffering is a sufficient rationale for your practice. In any case, the kindness of beings is not confined to their having been your mothers; their kindness to you was also powerful when they were enemies in providing you with an opportunity to practice patience. Furthermore, their kindness is not limited to a time when you are in the ordinary state; it also extends to you on the spiritual path, and even in the resultant state. It is only because of the existence of others that the buddhas can do beneficial work and engage in their noble activities.

Since you are equal to others in having the innate desire for happiness and in having natural rights to happiness and fortune, the only difference is the number of beings involved. When you talk of the welfare of yourself, that is only one; whereas when you talk of the welfare of others, that is a matter of an infinite number of beings. Naturally, the welfare of others is much more important than your own welfare. Through the practice of giving and taking, you will reach a state where you will spontaneously regard it as such.

The major instructions on generating the altruistic mind of bodhicitta—the seven-point cause and effect method and the equalizing and exchanging of oneself and others—could also be most effectively undertaken in combination. For such a combined practice, performed after the practitioner has laid within his or her mind the basis of equanimity, the sequence will be: (1) recognizing all beings as having been one's mother; (2) recollecting their kindness; (3) holding an uncommon recollection of kindness; (4) having the thought to repay their kindness; (5) developing loving kindness; (6) equalizing oneself and others; (7) reflecting on the disadvantages of the self-cherishing attitude; (8) reflecting on the advantages of the thought cherishing the welfare of others; (9) performing the actual exchange; (10) taking, concentrating on the aspirations of compassion; (11) giving, concentrating on the aspirations of love; (12) developing the special attitude; and the culmination, (13) achieving bodhicitta, the altruistic intention to attain enlightenment for the benefit of all.

By following the particular instructions in the *Bodhisattvacaryavatara*, you will be able to make gradual progress, eventually achieving a state where you will feel closer to other sentient beings and feel more and more distant from the self-cherishing attitude and selfish thoughts that are within, thus increasing the power and capacity of the altruism within you. This is how you should undertake the practice of bodhicitta.

13 Bodhisattva Vows Rite

The procedure for enhancing the generation of bodhicitta through ceremony is discussed next. One of the most effective factors for protecting the altruistic aspiration to attain enlightenment is mindfulness of the extensive benefits of bodhicitta.[32] In order to protect the mind from degeneration in future lifetimes, you should abstain from indulging in the four negative actions[33] and always adopt the four positive actions.[34]

To enhance and stabilize your generation of the bodhicitta mind, you should engage in the ceremony that reinforces its generation. It is recommended that mahayana practitioners take the bodhisattva vows, as doing this helps to generate a very strong sense of commitment to engage in the bodhisattva deeds.

In this text by Panchen Lobsang Choekyi Gyaltsen, the ceremony is performed on the basis of the verses quoted from *Bodhisattvacharyavatara*. According to this tradition, the ceremonies for generating both the aspirational and practical bodhicitta are explained in combination. However, because some masters like Gyaltsab-je and Panchen Sonam Drakpa have expressed qualms about the efficacy and the validity of such an approach, I prefer to conduct the ceremony based on Lama Tsongkhapa's commentary on the tenth chapter of *Bodhisattva Bhumi* entitled *Jhangchup Shunglam* (The Main Path to Enlightenment). Today the ceremony on taking the bodhisattva vows will be conducted according to the tradition of this text.

The practice of bodhicitta, exchanging and equalizing oneself with others, has been regarded as the core of all the practices of the Buddha by all the buddhas and the bodhisattvas of the past. In order to realize such an advanced state of the altruistic attitude within your mind, it is important to train your mind in the stages of the path explained in Lamrim texts in a properly graded course of application.

An effective method for reinforcing your training of the mind in the generation of bodhicitta is to repeatedly enhance it by taking the bodhicitta rite from your spiritual master. Doing so will have an added value, in that you are taking bodhisattva vows at the same time, thus making your generation of bodhicitta more powerful and inspired. The fact of participating in such a ceremony will act as a reminder in the future that, in the presence of a certain spiritual master, you have taken the altruistic commitment to work for the benefit of others.

As is written in sutras such as *Do-de Kelsang* (Sutra of Good Eon), many buddhas of the past have repeatedly generated bodhicitta in the presence of their spiritual masters. All the buddhas, the skillful, compassionate masters of the past, were originally ordinary beings like yourself; they took the initiative of generating bodhicitta in the presence of their masters and, having taken the solemn pledge, engaged in the practice.

You too have the potential within yourself to emulate their examples. Because your mind is changeable and has the nature of emptiness, you possess within yourself the buddha nature, the seed that allows for full enlightenment. Also, the essential nature of your mind is Clear Light, and the delusions that taint it are merely superficial and have not penetrated to its core. So, if you make the right effort, you have all the potentials within yourself to actualize the state of omniscience.

PRELIMINARIES

Today we are taking the bodhisattva vows. Some Tibetan masters of the past speak of different traditions of generating bodhicitta—according to the Madhyamika philosophical tenet system or the Cittamatrin system. But Lama Tsongkhapa maintains that so far as the ceremony for generating the altruistic aspiration of bodhicitta is concerned, there is no difference between the philosophical systems.

The ceremony is being conducted in the presence of a representative of Buddha Shakyamuni in the aspect of his image. Although we did not have the fortune to see Buddha Shakyamuni himself in person, we do have the great fortune of having access to his own precious teachings, which is actually superior to seeing him in person. The same is the case with great Indian masters like Nagarjuna and his immediate disciples. If we make the necessary effort, and undertake the practice and study, we can fully enjoy a benefit equal to that of having met them in person.

In Tibet, due to the profound kindness of the translators as well as that of the great religious kings, Tibetans had the good fortune and opportunity to undertake the practice and study of Buddhism without having to undergo the ordeals of traveling to India. On the basis of all these translations of the original Indian texts, many indigenous works later emerged, composed by masters of all the great traditions of Tibet. All this literature is at our disposal now.

So visualize in space, in front of you, all these exalted masters, including Buddha Shakyamuni, Nagarjuna, Aryadeva, and the eighty *mahasiddhas*; the great masters of the Nyingma tradition; Atisha and his followers, the masters of the Kadampa tradition; the five great masters of the Sakya tradition; the lineages of Lamdre practice; the great masters of the Kagyu lineage, such as Marpa, Milarepa, and their followers; and also the great masters of the Gelugpa lineage, Lama Tsongkhapa and his followers. Around you also are the protectors who have taken the oath in the presence of Buddha Shakyamuni to safeguard and protect the precious doctrine of Buddha. Visualize as well the harmful spirits—actually an embodiment of your own delusions—from which you are being protected by the guardians. Also visualize various emanations of the buddhas actively working for the benefit of all living beings. Surrounding you are all sentient beings in the aspect of human beings, though undergoing the sufferings of their individual realms of existence. Now generate a strong force of compassion directed towards all these sentient beings, particularly your enemies.

Having created this mental image, question yourself as to how all these objects of refuge, the buddhas and the masters of the past, achieved such a high state of realization and reached a state where they can provide protection to all living beings. You will find that it is because of their having made effort in the practice of dharma in general and, in particular, the practice of bodhicitta. Think as follows: "I shall, from today, follow in the footsteps of these great masters, and take the initiative of generating bodhicitta."

Strictly speaking, a practitioner who is taking the bodhisattva vows should have as a prerequisite the aspirational attitude of bodhicitta. Although it is very rare, some among you might have it; but for the majority of us it is very difficult to possess such a genuine and non-simulated bodhicitta. As we discussed earlier, altruism or good heart is the source of all goodness and benefit. Therefore, although we may not have realized a genuine bodhicitta within ourselves, at least we should have a very strong single-pointed admiration for it and simulate the experience of an altruistic mind.

The person from whom you are taking the bodhisattva vows should have the realization of bodhicitta, and such a master should also be an expert in the rite of giving the bodhisattva vows. Although I do not claim to have the full qualifications myself, I can quite confidently say that I do have a very strong admiration for the observance of the noble ideals of a bodhisattva. I have received the bodhisattva vows myself according to the procedure outlined in this text from my tutor, the late Kyabje Ling Rinpoche, at the sacred site of the Bodh Gaya stupa. Today the bodhisattva vows are being imparted to you through the same ceremony.

Initial request to the preceptor
[The ceremony begins with a request to the master to bestow the vows. When you make the request, you should kneel and bow down to the master. Those who cannot kneel can sit, but those who can should maintain a kneeling position.]
Repeat the following request three times:

O my master, pray attend to me.
I, a child of the family, seek to take the vows of bodhisattva ethics; should there be no harm kindly listen to my plea and bestow the vows.

[The master then, quoting heavily from the sutras and related commentaries by great bodhisattvas, explains the great benefits of bodhicitta in order to inspire you to rejoice in having the fortune of obtaining this precious opportunity to take the bodhisattva vows and firmly commit yourself to the noble ideals of the bodhisattvas.

Then the guru advises that your motive for taking the bodhisattva vows should be right and altruistic. He does this by asking you the following questions:]

O child of the family, listen to me.
Do you aspire to liberate the beings who are not liberated yet, free those who are not free yet, relieve those not relieved yet, and lead to the state beyond sorrow those who have not reached that state yet? Do you desire that the lineage of Buddha not cease? If so, you must stabilize your generation of the altruistic mind and reaffirm your pledge.

[Sit down.]

Accumulation of merit
To amass vast stores of merit you should reflect upon the great advantages and benefits of taking the bodhisattva vows. Visualize all the buddhas, bodhisattvas, and masters above in space. In their presence, with mindfulness upon their great exceptional qualities, cultivate strong faith in them while main-

taining your perception of your own spiritual master, who is
conducting the ceremony, as a real living buddha.

Undertake the seven-limbed practice—prostration, making
offerings, and so forth. When you recite the verses of the seven-
limbed practice, do so slowly, reflecting upon the meaning of
each verse, contemplating the exceptional qualities of the body,
speech, and mind of the buddhas. While developing faith from
the depth of your mind, sing the praises of these buddhas.
Follow this with confession, admiration for your virtues, sup-
plication to the spiritual masters to turn the wheel of the
dharma, and dedication. As explained earlier, visualize the
buddhas and bodhisattvas in front and above you in space and
yourself surrounded by all living beings in the aspect of human beings. Think that as a preliminary to taking the vows
you shall engage in the seven-limbed practice. With such reflections, recite the following verses of the seven-limbed practice:

> O Lions amongst men,
> Buddhas past, present and future,
> To as many of you as exist in the ten directions,
> I bow down with body, speech, and mind.
>
> On waves of strength of this king
> Of praises of exalted, sublime ways,
> With bodies numerous as atoms of the world,
> I bow down to the Buddhas pervading space.
>
> On every atom is found a Buddha
> Sitting amidst countless bodhisattvas.
> In this infinite sphere of mystic beings,
> I gaze with eyes of faith.
>
> With oceans of every possible sound
> In eulogy of the perfect Buddhas,
> I give voice to their excellent qualities:
> Hail those passed to bliss.

Garlands of supreme flowers I offer them;
And beautiful sounds, supreme parasols,
Butter lamps and sacred incense,
I offer to all Awakened Ones.

Excellent food, supreme fragrance,
And a mound of powders as high as Meru
I arrange in mystic formation
And offer to those who have conquered themselves.

All these peerless offerings I hold up
In admiration for those gone to bliss.
In accord with exalted and sublime ways,
I prostrate and make offerings to the Buddhas.

Whatever ill deeds I have committed,
Under the power of desire, anger and ignorance,
Through my body, speech and mind,
I confess and purify these individually.

In the merits of all sentient beings,
Solitary realizers, learners and those beyond learning,
Buddhas in ten directions and their heirs,
I rejoice in all their virtues.

O, the light of all universes in ten directions,
Who realized Buddhahood through the stages of
    enlightenment.
I appeal to all of you, protectors,
To turn the unsurpassed wheel.

I entreat with folded hands
Those intending to enter nirvana
To live for eons equal to the atoms on earth,
For the benefit and happiness of all beings.

Whatever little merit that I have accumulated,
Through prostrating, offering, confessing,
Rejoicing, requesting, and entreating,
I dedicate all towards attaining full enlightenment.

Let us undertake the confession of negativities, as Gung-thang Tenpai Dronme recommended in one of his writings, in conjunction with the recitation of the *Confession Sutra*. While reciting, reaffirm your visualization of the buddhas and bodhisattvas and yourself being surrounded by suffering sentient beings. The factors that obstruct you in accomplishing what you most seek to do—that is, work for the benefit of other sentient beings—is your self-cherishing attitude and the negativities that you have committed, forced by your selfish thoughts. When doing this recitation, let us stand up and do prostrations in unison. While prostrating, recite the *Confession Sutra*.

An urgent request for the vows
[Resume the kneeling position and make the following request three times:]

O master, kindly bestow upon me the perfect vows of
bodhisattva ethics; do bestow them quickly.

Rejoicing
Having made this request, you should now solemnly sit down on your cushions with a feeling of joy at the immediate prospect of receiving the vows.

Determining the presence of any obstacles
[In order to examine if you are adequately qualified to take the vows, the master asks the following:]

O child of the family and spiritual brother/sister, called
[...(insert name)], are you a bodhisattva? And did
you make aspirational prayers for enlightenment?

Reply by saying: "Yes, I have."

[Then the master asks further:]

Do you wish to receive from me the ethics of the bodhisattva and also all the basis of bodhisattva training?

Reply: "Yes, I do."

THE MAIN RITE

Now the actual ceremony of conferring the vows begins. Reaffirm the visualization of buddhas and bodhisattvas in the
space in front of you, and of yourself being surrounded by
all sentient beings. Then reflect: "Although I too am still in
the cycle of existence, tormented by delusions and sufferings,
I am much more fortunate than many of these sentient beings, in that I have obtained a human existence and possess
the capacity to judge between what is beneficial and what is
harmful. Therefore, being always mindful of the great preciousness of bodhicitta, I will determine that I will work for
the attainment of the completely enlightened state for the benefit of all. I will, by taking the bodhisattva vows, dedicate my
whole life and energy to the practical application of the noble
ideals of the bodhisattva."

Those among you who do not feel committed enough to engage in the bodhisattva deeds should not take the bodhisattva
vows. Develop, instead, the altruistic attitude, "May I achieve
the completely enlightened state for the benefit of all beings."

But those who do feel enough commitment should take the
bodhisattva vows and make the following pledge:

Just as the great bodhisattvas of the past first generated bodhicitta, took the vows and dedicated themselves to the bodhisattva deeds, I too will take the
vows and observe them by engaging in the bodhisattva deeds.

The preceptor asks you the following three times; after each
question, reply positively. When you finish the third repeti-

tion, strongly imagine that you have received the complete set of bodhisattva vows.[35]

> O [...(insert name of the disciple)], child of the family, will you take from me the bodhisattva's morality of restraint, the morality of gathering virtue, and the morality of working for others' welfare, in short all the ethical codes of bodhisattvas and their practices, which were the basis for the training of all the bodhisattvas of the past, and are for all those present, and will ever remain so for all future bodhisattvas?

Reply: "Yes, I will."

CONCLUDING RITES

Evoking the attention of the buddhas
[When the preceptor, while reciting the following, calls for the kind attention of all the buddhas in the ten directions, imagine yourself touching, with your head, the feet of the buddhas and bodhisattvas visualized in front of you.]

> O, I beseech the attention of all the buddhas who, though residing in countless realms in the ten directions and being beyond ordinary comprehension, possess the mind from which no event or sentient being is concealed. I call to your kind attention that Bodhisattva [...(insert name of the disciple)] has taken the perfect vows of a bodhisattva three times from me, Bodhisattva [...(insert the name of the preceptor)]; and I bear witness to this event.

Words of encouragement through explaining the benefits
[The preceptor now gives you encouragement by explaining the great benefits of having taken the vows and generated the practical aspects of bodhicitta.]
Bodhisattvacharyavatara says that the power of generating

the practical aspect of the mind is such that once you have generated it through taking the vows, even when you are asleep your store of merit will continue to increase.

Lama Tsongkhapa says in his text that the moment we have taken the bodhisattva vows, the buddhas in all the directions will have an indication of the great event and will bear witness to our taking the vows. They will perceive that on such and such a day—for example, today—in this Himalayan region of Dharamsala, inside Thekchen Choeling temple, many disciples headed by Ven. Lobsang Nyima, Jhangtse Choje [one of the two high masters next in the line of Tsongkhapa's throne] took the bodhisattva vows from the Bhikshu Tenzin Gyatso. Because of this, the buddhas will pray for the success of these bodhisattvas and always sustain them as their own children.

The bodhisattva vows are superior to many other forms of vows. Taking them constitutes the accumulation of great stores of merit and also protects the practitioner from many negative actions.

Do not speak unnecessarily of the bodhisattva vows to untrained ones and those who have no faith in the bodhisattva practices. Doing so can be harmful for the listener who does not appreciate the bodhisattva principles; such persons may speak against the bodhisattva vows, and thus indulge in grave negative actions. Therefore, when speaking about the bodhisattva vows it is crucial to judge the suitability of the listener.

Offering of thanks
[The ceremony concludes with the offerings of thanks. Both the master and the disciples make offerings to all the buddhas and bodhisattvas. This should be done by reciting the verses of the seven-limbed practice (see pages 180–82 above).

14 The Bodhisattva Deeds

Generating an altruistic attitude alone is not enough—you should engage in the bodhisattva deeds after having made your pledge, because without the deeds you have only an altruistic attitude. Without engaging in the bodhisattva deeds, you will not be able to achieve the omniscient state, the attainment of which is so vital for the work of benefiting others to your fullest capacity.

The bodhisattva deeds or way of life must accord with the principles you adopted when first generating the altruistic mind of bodhicitta—the commitment to work for the welfare of all beings. Therefore, the ultimate object of aspiration of a bodhisattva is the attainment of the form body of a buddha, because it is only in the aspect of the form body that buddhas are able to teach sentient beings and work for the benefit of others. Such a form body can be achieved by totally eliminating the obstructions to knowledge. You have to develop the Clear Light mind within yourself to the fullest extent to make it omniscient, since without the achievement of omniscience, you will not be able to achieve the form bodies of the buddhas. At the resultant state, there are two kayas or bodies—the sublime truth body (dharmakaya) and the sublime form body (rupakaya).

The bodhisattva has to engage in a path that has the complete aspects of method and wisdom leading to such a resultant state. This path is that of the union of method and wisdom, or in other words, the accumulations of merit and wisdom. The practices of method and wisdom should be undertaken not in isolation, but rather in union. The practice of wisdom is constituted by the accumulation of wisdom, whereas all the other practices such as bodhicitta, generosity, morality, and so forth are practices that accumulate stores of merit.

THE SIX PERFECTIONS

The application of bodhicitta can be done through the study and practice of the six perfections.

1 Generosity

The first among the six perfections is generosity. Generosity is of three types: giving material aid, giving dharma, and protecting from fear. "Giving dharma" refers to the giving of teachings to other sentient beings out of the pure motivation to benefit them. The phrase does not only refer to high lamas giving teachings seated on high thrones. You should not have the notion that dharma teachings should be preceded by impressive rituals such as the blowing of conch shells and the like. Rather, any instruction given out of compassion and a kind heart by anyone is considered generosity of the dharma.

Giving away one's own possessions without even the slightest touch of miserliness and without any hope for reward is part of the practice of generosity. It would be very beneficial, if you want to practice generosity, to make offerings to sick patients and also to the monastic universities which have philosophical study programs and which train many young monks for the practice of dharma.

The practice of generosity should be undertaken by giving away what you can afford. You should enhance and develop your thought of generosity to such an extent that eventually

you will be able to part with even your own body which you
hold most precious, without the slightest trace of apprehension or possessiveness. As in any practice, it is important right
from the beginning never to be discouraged, never to think
that you will not be able to do it.

Protecting someone from fear or danger is the giving of fearlessness, as is saving people from illness and so forth. The practice of rituals for the purpose of overcoming illness could also
justifiably be called the giving of fearlessness. But genuine practitioners of dharma who emphasize the practice of Lamrim
and thought transformation should basically not have precon-
ceptions that suffering is caused by such and such a spirit.
Although the latter is possible, basically one's own karmic actions are responsible for one's harm and suffering. If you have
definite indications of being harmed by certain spirits, then—
instead of doing all these rituals—the most effective way to overcome the difficulty is to practice compassion towards the forces
that harm you. Such occasions give you new opportunities to
practice your compassion, which is far more powerful than performing rituals.

Although we Tibetans talk about the law of cause and effect and the Buddha's doctrine, when a difficult situation really
presses us we often like to blame it on the harm of spirits.
It is far better to have fewer superstitions and more faith in
the law of causality.

However, if many internal and external signs indicate that
harm is caused by spirits, then there are certain rituals actually recommended by the Buddha himself to overcome the
problem. If these rituals can be practiced properly, benefit will
ensue. The monks performing the rituals should do so on the
basis of divine identity with a meditational deity and a very
strong motivation of altruism.

2   *Morality*

Next is the practice of morality. If you have taken monastic
vows, observe them properly and live up to the standards of
the Buddha's bhikshus. You should never follow the example

of corrupted monks. In the world there are people who even go to the extent of killing their parents. The fact that there are people who do this does not mean you should follow their example. Similarly, although within the Buddhist community there are monks who are unbecoming in their way of life, you should rather follow the example of good and perfect monks. It is better to have a lesser number with better quality than a greater number with inferior quality.

Lay people should engage in the practice of morality by abstaining from the ten negative actions—if possible, all ten. But if this is not possible, then at least taking the life of others, telling lies, and indulging in sexual misconduct should be avoided; these are very detrimental, not only for the individual but also for the peace and calmness of a community. Divisive talk is very destructive; it causes a lot of conflict and misunderstanding within a community, and between different communities and different people. Therefore, it is a great obstacle to peace and happiness of mind. The same is true of telling lies. Senseless gossip, although not so destructive from one point of view, is seen from another to be very harmful, as it wastes so much of your precious time. You should also avoid harsh speech and covetousness, as well as harmful intent and holding perverted views. "Perverted views" refers to incorrect views that deny the existence of life after death and the law of causality.

Also, as Nagarjuna recommends in his *Ratnavali* (Precious Garland), it is important to avoid taking alcoholic drinks. In Tibet, because of the lack of relaxation available under the repressive Chinese rule, some people indulge in taking alcohol, which is very injurious. Buddha himself has said that those who regard him as their master should never take an alcoholic drink, even as little as fits on the tip of a blade of grass.

Gambling is also very injurious; it involves all sorts of negative actions like telling lies, being covetous, and using harsh speech. Because many negative actions ensue from gambling, Nagarjuna taught that gambling is very destructive.

The same is true of smoking. Even the modern doctors speak

of the destructive effect of smoking on one's health. Smoking is an addiction; it is not as if we could not survive if we did not smoke. Nor is it like taking tea. Because tea is a key part of our diet, if we are told by the doctor not to drink it, we have to find something as an alternative. But smoking is completely different: we do not need to smoke at all. Because of their misconceptions and the bad habit of smoking, some people even find the smell of tobacco quite nice. Smoking is very bad for the purse, too. Rather than smoke, it would be better to go for a picnic and enjoy a nice lunch or dinner. This is not religious talk—the issue is one of health. It would be better right from the beginning not to indulge in and develop the addiction to tobacco.

3 *Patience*

There are different types of patience: the patience of being indifferent to the harm inflicted by others, the patience of voluntarily accepting hardship, and the patience developed through reasoned conviction in the dharma. Practitioners of dharma should have these types of patience—they should be able to endure hardship—but adopting such patience does not mean that they should not take precautions for their health.

When you have a sickness, right from the beginning it is better to treat it by going to doctors and taking medicine. It is no good leaving matters to the last moment, which is, in part, a habit of Tibetans. Because in Tibet there were very few doctors, when someone became sick, people would advise the person to take more food and have a good rest. This is inadequate advice. It is more important to look into the causes of the illness and apply corrective measures. Taking care of your health is very important, particularly for meditators in the high mountains and for students in the monastic communities who have to undergo very rigorous training.

At the same time, meditators and students should have the patience which can voluntarily accept hardship; without such patience they will never be successful in their studies. Gung-thang Jampeyang said:

Should you wish to be learned in the ways of avoid-
ing delusions and attaining liberation,
And achieve the glory of an eloquent scholar confi-
dent amidst any assembly,
Accept with patience the hardships involved.
For the leisurely lifestyle of the present,
Totally attached to the pleasures of delicacies, drinks
and excessive sleep,
Will get you nowhere.

Similarly, the patience of being indifferent to harm inflicted
by others is especially important for practitioners of Mahayana,
because Mahayana doctrine in particular and Buddha's doctrine in general are rooted in compassion. Therefore, you should
be able to forbear and endure the harm inflicted by others.
Buddha said that those who retaliate against harm inflicted by
others are not his followers. You should also view all the harm
that you face and that is inflicted by others—as well as the adverse circumstances that you experience—as a manifestation
and ripening of your own negative actions. Doing this will enable you to endure the suffering with greater patience. When
facing difficulties such as illnesses and adverse circumstances,
it is very important to reflect on the law of causality, and conclude that these are the consequences of your own doings in
the past.

This conclusion will protect you from having all sorts of superstitions or unnecessary mental anxieties, but this does not
mean that you should not work toward the relief of the
problems.

Some people misunderstand the concept of karma. They take
the Buddha's doctrine of the law of causality to mean that all
is predetermined, that there is nothing that the individual can
do. This is a total misunderstanding. The very term karma
or action is a term of active force, which indicates that future
events are within your own hands. Since action is a phenomenon that is committed by a person, a living being, it is within
your own hands whether or not you engage in actions.

There are differing techniques for various types of practitioners. For some it is effective, when facing adverse circumstances, to reflect that these are due to the nature of suffering and are the natural consequences of being in the cycle of existence. Others could view adverse circumstances as the ripening of their own negative actions and could wish that by the experience of these sufferings all other sentient beings will never undergo such experiences in the future.

4   *Joyous Effort*

If one has the faculty of joyous effort, one will be able to accomplish the task that one has originally set out to do. Therefore, this faculty is very important for a spiritual practitioner. Generally speaking, there are three types of joyous effort: (1) armor-like joyous effort; (2) joyous effort in gathering virtues; and (3) joyous effort in working for others. The main obstacles to the development of these efforts are the different levels of laziness—primarily the laziness of procrastination, and the lazinesses stemming from indolence and from a sense of inferiority.[36]

5   *Concentration*

Since the practices of concentration and wisdom are treated in separate chapters, only a brief explanation of these is given here.

Generally speaking, concentration refers to a faculty of single-pointedness of the mind that serves as a powerful basis for any given meditation. It is of two types, based on differing functions: mundane and super-mundane concentrations.

6   *Wisdom*

Wisdom refers to an analytic faculty of the mind that allows a probing into the deeper nature of things. Broadly speaking, it is of two kinds: the wisdom examining the ultimate nature of phenomena, and the wisdom examining the conventional or relative nature of phenomena.

THE FOUR RIPENING FACTORS

The four ripening factors refer to the four principal factors that bodhisattvas employ in attracting disciples and enhancing their spiritual potentials. These are: (1) giving material aid; (2) speaking eloquently; (3) always giving the right counsel; and (4) setting an example by living the principles taught. It is through these skillful means that the compassionate bodhisattvas work for the welfare of all other beings.

15 Calm Abiding of Mind

Concentration is a very important factor for the completion of the practice of wisdom. First of all, the practitioner should accumulate the conditions for a perfect practice of single-pointedness. Samadhi or concentration practice is common to both Buddhists and non-Buddhists; without such a faculty you will not be able to make great progress in the spiritual path—it is indispensable. Particularly for people like us who are engaged in the practice of a union of sutra and tantra, and particularly highest yoga tantra, it is very important to have single-pointed concentration, a faculty that will enable us to channel all our energy on a chosen object.

The appropriate conditions for undertaking the practice of single-pointedness of the mind, or in other words, calm abiding, are a conducive environment, fewer excessive activities, study of the text related to the practice of calm abiding, no unnecessary meetings with people, adoption of the right physical posture, and so forth.

For the actual practice of calm abiding, various objects can be taken as the focus of meditation, such as a pebble, a piece of wood or any other object. But for an added advantage, it is very good to take the image of a buddha as an object of meditation. We who are engaged in the practice of deity yoga can visualize the object of meditation above in the space in front of us, or visualize a replica of the spiritual master at our crowns dissolving into us, and then ourselves transforming into the image of Buddha Shakyamuni. Seated in a vajrasana (cross-legged) position, we can do these visualizations—either we see the object of visualization in front of us or, if we have taken tantric initiations, we can visualize ourselves in the aspect of Buddha Shakyamuni.

As I remarked earlier, for some practitioners it is better to visualize with closed eyes, but for others—although it is diffi-cult at the beginning—it is more effective and yields better results in the future if they can develop the habit of doing medi-tation with open eyes. Otherwise, if they start meditating with closed eyes, the moment they open their eyes their minds are easily distracted. Another point to note is that since you are cultivating calm abiding and single-pointedness on the basis of the mental consciousness and not on the sensory level, it is good to try to develop the habit of doing meditation with open eyes, totally neglecting the visual consciousness. In this way, you will get to a point where you will be able to prevent the conditions that give rise to an active visual consciousness.

Now, when you actually engage in the meditation of calm abiding, channeling your mind on a given object and main-taining single-pointedness, if your chosen object, such as a color, changes into a different color, you should try to reaf-firm your visualization of the color that you originally chose. You should not let your mind come under the control of the distraction.

Right from the beginning it is important that you have a very strong determination that—even if it means having only a short session—you shall conduct a perfect meditation, one totally free from the influences of mental sinking and mental excitement, and never deviating from the chosen object of medi-tation.

Then, while in the actual meditation session it is crucial never to lose the object of meditation that you have chosen. When the mind is focused and directed upon this object, it should be relaxed, but if it is too relaxed there is a danger of mental sinking creeping in. Therefore, you should have a certain degree of intensity while maintaining single-pointedness, as though your mind had fused with the chosen object. This combination of intensity and relaxed alertness is essential. When you have it, the mental clarity of your meditation will increase, whereas if you try to have too relaxed a state of mind right from the beginning, you will be prevented from making progress in your meditation.

If you want to engage in a perfect meditation of calm abiding, with a single-pointed concentration, you should apply the eight opponent forces to overcome the five main obstacles to the attainment of a single-pointedness of mind. One obstacle is laziness. To overcome it, there are four opponent forces: faith in the value of meditative single-pointedness; deep interest in and admiration for the practice of single-pointedness due to seeing its benefits; joyous effort; and mental pliancy. Recollection of mindfulness is the opponent force for losing your object of meditation.

Mental alertness or introspection detects the arisal of mental sinking and mental excitement. This faculty of introspection is of vital importance.

There are many different levels of practitioners. Some whose introspection is very powerful will be able to prevent even the arisal of mental sinking right from the beginning, receiving a kind of forewarning when the mental faults are about to arise. But those whose practice of introspection is not very strong will be able to stop the sinking only after it has already arisen. There are different levels of mental sinking—some are gross and some are subtle. The cause for the arisal of mental sinking is that the mind is too relaxed; in order to overcome that you should reinforce the intensity of your mind and alertness. This can be done by reflecting upon things that are joyful and admirable—such as the great qualities of the Buddha's body, speech and mind—or by visualizing a bright light, or by imagining your mind springing into space and becoming infused with it. Such types of visualization are effective in overcoming mental sinking.

Another fault that obstructs the cultivation of single-pointedness is that of mental excitement and scattering. It arises when the mind is distracted to external objects. In order to overcome it, it is effective to employ visualizations that will enable you to withdraw your mind within and feel a sense of renunciation. Reflecting upon impermanence and the faults and miserable state of cyclic existence is effective.

The unnecessary application of antidotes or opponent forces when there is no mental sinking or excitement at all is also an obstacle; therefore, you should cultivate equanimity, which is non-application of opponent forces when there is no arisal of mental sinking or excitement.

All these obstacles to meditation will arise differently, according to the variations in age, mental faculty, experience, and mental disposition of the practitioners. Therefore, you should judge for yourself how best to cope with them. The point is that you have to maintain equilibrium or a balanced state of mental intensity and single-pointedness, so that your mind is not under the influence of either mental sinking or excitement. You should not be satisfied with having just a stable visualization alone; there should be clarity and intensity of the subjective experience as well. The image should be both clear and stable.

When you undertake the practice of single-pointedness by applying the eight opponent forces,[37] you will be able to realize the nine mental stages[38] and be thus led to a perfect calm abiding.

Sometimes—as Lama Tsongkhapa recommended in his shorter version of Lamrim, or as the Panchen Lama stated in his commentary on mahamudra—since a tantric practitioner's ultimate aim is to withdraw all the energy winds and gross levels of mind into the subtle mind and wind, cultivating calm abiding by taking your own mind as the object of meditation is very powerful and will yield additional benefit in the future.

16 *Wisdom Through Special Insight*

The next practice is that of wisdom, based on the cultivation of vipassana or special insight. When you undertake the practice of special insight you should visualize your spiritual guru in the aspect of Manjushri and make the request.

The actual meditation on special insight is explained here in terms of meditation on the identity-lessness or selflessness of persons and the selflessness of phenomena. When the self-grasping attitude arises within you, it is the self-grasping attitude focused upon phenomena that arises first and that leads to the egoistic attitude of grasping at the inherent existence of your own self. However, when you do the meditation, because of the significance of the objects on which you qualify the emptiness, meditation on the selflessness of persons prior to meditation on the selflessness of phenomena will prove more effective and powerful.

SELFLESSNESS OF PERSONS

To do the meditation on the selflessness of persons, think that the self or person is nothing other than a label imputed on the composite of physical and mental aggregates. As Nagarjuna explains in his *Ratnavali*:

> A person is not the earth, nor water,
> Nor wind, nor space.
> Neither is it consciousness, nor all of them;
> Yet apart from these what person is there?

For example, right now you feel that you are sitting on the mat, but now search for that self or person. You will find that it is not to be found in the physical or mental aggregates. It is none of the four elements, such as the elemental particles that form the body. These elements cannot be posited as persons from their own side; the collection of them is not the person; nor are they individually the person. The person is only a label imputed on the aggregation of all these designative bases, and therefore it exists only nominally. There is no such person that exists inherently, truly, and independently.

The tradition explains that undertaking the analysis on the emptiness of inherent existence with the four essential points is very powerful and effective. These points are (1) identifying the object of negation, (2) ascertaining the pervasion, (3) ascertaining the absence of singularity, and (4) ascertaining the absence of plurality.

The first essential point is identifying the object of negation. We all possess within ourselves an innate notion of self as existing inherently and as something self-evident. Especially when very powerful emotions arise, for example when you are accused by others, then you feel your ''self'' very strongly. Under such circumstances, you will have an intense feeling of I-ness or selfhood. At that point you should immediately try to see, from a corner of your mind, how that self or the person appears to you and how you relate to it.

Then you will be able to identify the mode of apprehension of the innate self-grasping attitude and how the person, your own I, appears to that consciousness. The natural attitude apprehends a self existing inherently, truly, and totally independently of the body and mind. You will find that it is as if there is a person or self that is like a master dominating the body and mind—a totally independent entity, that seems to solidly exist. On the basis of such a misconception, all the negative emotions such as desire and hatred arise.

If you undertake the meditation described above, you will be able to identify the self as apprehended by this misconception quite clearly, through your own experience. When you do this analysis, you will get to a state where you will feel rather impatient at being unable to locate the self or person at all and will conclude that you are forced to posit the person as existing merely on a nominal level.

It is important to relate all this analysis to your own way of thinking. You can reason that if things, the self or the person, exist as they appear to you, when you analytically search for the essence behind the label you should be able to find it. But you cannot find it; as a result of your analysis you end with seeing through the deception of your misconception! If you follow the instructions on the analytic examination as explained in this text, identification of the self as apprehended by the misconceived attitude will become clearer. That is the essential point of identifying the object of negation.

The second essential point is the ascertainment of pervasion. Pervasion refers to an element of the logic of necessity that one finds underlying phenomena. In the present context, it is the premise that if anything exists inherently and objectively in its own right, then it should do so as either inherently one or multiple, with no third possibility, just as everything that exists at the relative level does so either as a single entity or a multiple. Thus, if the self exists as apprehended by this misconception—as totally independent or inherently existing within and amidst the body and the mind, the aggregates—then the self or the person should exist either as one with the aggregates or as totally separate from them. Since single and multiple form a dichotomy and there is no third possibility, these two together observe the law of the excluded middle. That is how you ascertain the essential point of pervasion.

The third essential point is that of ascertaining the absence of singularity. This is done by analyzing whether or not the self or person exists as single or totally one with the aggregates. If the self exists as single or totally one with the aggregates, then the contradiction arises that just as the aggregates are many, the self should also be multiple. Also, when this present life ceases at the time of death, the continuity of the self should also cease right then. And, if the self or the person is totally one with the aggregates, how can one have the natural feeling of the self being the master of these aggregates and the aggregates being the subjects and possessions of that self? Furthermore, how can one logically maintain that the basis of designation and the designation itself are one and the same thing?

To ascertain the absence of plurality, consider that if the self or the person exists independently, separate from the aggregates, then after mentally disintegrating the aggregates one should be able to point out a self or person existing independent of these aggregates—but one cannot. If the self or the person is a totally different and separate entity from the aggregates, then there should be no relation between the self and the aggregates at all.

Thus, when you analytically probe in such a manner, you will not find the person or the self: the person or self cannot withstand the analysis of such an ultimate scrutiny. If the person existed independently, truly, and inherently, then it should be able to withstand any form of ultimate analysis. When you employ such an examination or analysis you will be able to reach a state where the self as apprehended and perceived by your misconception does not exist. And you will really begin to question the validity of your natural tendency to believe in an inherently existent I or self, which you take to be such a self-evident phenomenon.

Just as Lama Tsongkhapa explains in his *Gongpa Rabsel,* a commentary on *Madhyamikavatara,* you will come to the conclusion that the self or the person is a mere label imputed upon the basis of the aggregates. Gaining such an understanding constitutes a realization of the selflessness of persons. When such a realization is maintained and reinforced through constant meditation and familiarization, you will be able to develop it into an intuitive or direct experience.

Within the selflessness of persons there are many different levels, some that are gross. A gross level of selflessness of persons is the person as not existing substantially, or not having a self-sufficient identity. If any level or degree of selflessness, once having been realized upon the person, brings you the realization of emptiness when applied to other phenomena, then it is a genuine understanding of the subtle selflessness of persons. An understanding of all these different levels of selflessness is very important for leading you to the final and ultimate nature of things, emptiness.

Having developed certainty and ascertainment in your realization of the non-inherent existence of the person and the realization of the person as a mere label imputed upon the designative bases, the mind-body collection, you should maintain a meditative equipoise. When the ascertainment becomes weaker, you should reaffirm it by applying the analytic process as before. During meditative equipoise it is important to keep your concentration deeply absorbed on the mere absence and total negation of the inherent existence of the person, without having any speculation as to any implication of another level of existence.

It is during the post-meditational period that the meditator will be led to the realization of the conventional reality of phenomena. Although phenomena lack inherent existence, still they have a certain level of existence which, you can conclude, is only conventional and relative. Thus, you will be able to perceive all phenomena as if they were illusions. There is no need to make an extra effort to have such a realization: If your understanding of non-inherent existence or emptiness is perfect during meditative equipoise, then during the post-meditational period the understanding of the illusion-like nature of conventional reality—the fact that although phenomena appear in one way they exist in another—will come naturally as a by-product.

SELFLESSNESS OF PHENOMENA

The meditation on the selflessness of phenomena is divided into two: meditating upon the selflessness of compounded phenomena and meditating upon the selflessness of uncompounded phenomena. Just as the person or the self lacks inherent existence, all one's belongings and the environment and phenomena lack inherent existence.

The category of compounded phenomena is divided into three: matter, consciousness, and abstract but transitory phenomena. The first, matter, includes the body. When you think of the body you ordinarily have the natural feeling that the different parts—such as the head, arms, and so forth—exist independently, or have an inherent existence, from their own side. This feeling is not valid: when you analyze the parts of the body, you will find that they are just mere labels imputed upon the aggregation of their designative bases, their own parts.

You should also apply the same process of analysis to the body as a whole—is the body totally one with its parts or is it totally independent and separate from its parts?—and to external phenomena like houses, towns, mountains, trees, forests, and so forth. What is a forest? Is it the collection of all the trees or the individual trees themselves? You will find that forest is a mere label imputed upon the collection of all these different trees. Similarly, the various qualities—good, bad, long, short, tall—are relative terms imputed in relation to something else. This shows their nature of dependence. There is no independently and inherently existing long or short that is an absolute in itself.

The same form of analysis should also address the topic of consciousness. Consider whether or not consciousness exists independently and inherently, and then whether consciousness is one with the consciousness of an earlier instance or is totally separate from it.

The third category of compounded phenomena is that of abstract but transitory phenomena. This term refers to phenomena such as time, year, month, day, and so forth which are not tangible. If a year existed independently, then it would not depend upon its parts, such as the months. But without depending upon months, how can one posit a year? So year is nothing other than a label imputed upon the collection of a number of months. The same kind of analysis should be extended to uncompounded phenomena, such as space, as well. Nagarjuna said in his *Mulamadhyamika Karika* (Fundamental Treatise on the Middle Way): "If things compounded are not established, how can those that are non-compounded be established?"

In short, you should be able to get to a realization that not only your own person but also all phenomena lack inherent existence and are illusory in the sense that, although they appear to be truly existent, they lack such a status.

Thus meditate upon the emptiness of all phenomena. Meditation on the emptiness of non-compounded phenomena is very important, especially a focus on the non-inherent existence of emptiness itself. This is because there is a grave danger of falling into the trap of conceiving emptiness as truly existent. Having negated the true existence of all other phenomena, you might tend to apprehend emptiness itself as being truly existent, because it is the ultimate nature. Just as all phenomena lack true existence or inherent existence, so does emptiness. There is no independent emptiness or inherently existent emptiness that is not dependent upon the subject which it qualifies. Emptiness is always a quality or a property, and there is no emptiness which can exist independently, without a basis on which it is qualified.

Therefore, emptiness is a mere label imputed upon a basis, as, for example, the emptiness of vase is nothing other than the ultimate nature of vase. The very absence or negation of the inherent existence of the vase is emptiness. Just as the subject *vase* is empty, so too is the quality emptiness.

Overcoming the misapprehension of emptiness as truly existent is crucial. Many texts speak of this misconception as an irreparable view. Because there is a great danger of misapprehending emptiness as truly existent, the sutras mention many synonyms for the emptiness of emptiness: the emptiness of ultimate nature, the emptiness of ultimate truth, and so forth. The explanations of all these are designed to overcome the misapprehension of emptiness as truly existent.

Realization of such an emptiness through analysis both during meditative equipoise and the post-meditational periods, when accompanied by a physical and mental pliancy achieved through calm abiding meditation, marks the attainment of special insight focused on emptiness.

17 *Tantra in Context*

Having trained your mind in the common paths of Lamrim, you should engage in the practice of tantra, which is the gateway of the fortunate ones. It is by engaging in such a powerful and sophisticated path that the practitioner will be able to expedite his or her accumulation of merit and wisdom and achieve omniscience within the shortest possible time.

With that, this brief experiential commentary on Panchen Lama Lobsang Choekyi Gyaltsen's *Lamrim* is concluded. As I have remarked over the last few days, the essence of the Buddha's doctrine is to be a kind and good human being and to practice altruism.

Appendix I
Commitments and Precepts of Thought Transformation Practice

COMMITMENTS OF THOUGHT TRANSFORMATION PRACTICE

1. Do not disregard or contradict any pledges that you have made.

2. Do not allow your thought transformation practice to increase arrogance.

3. Do not let yourself fall into partiality towards others.

4. Maintain a natural external behavior acceptable to others, while internally transforming your mind.

5. Do not speak of the faults of others.

6. Do not think of others' failings, even when you see them.

7. Apply antidotes to the delusions that are strongest in you with greater emphasis.

8. Give up all hope for personal reward for your thought tranformation practice.

9. Do not let your positive actions be polluted by the poisons of the self-cherishing attitude and by thoughts that grasp at the inherent existence of things.

10. Hold no grudge towards those who cause harm.

11. Do not respond in kind when scolded by others.

12. Do not retaliate in return when harmed by others.

13. Abstain from any actions harmful to others' bodies or minds.

14. Do not blame others for your own shortcomings and failures.

15. Abandon selfish motives of appropriating the belongings of a community for your personal gain.

16. Do not undertake the thought transformation practice merely because of the wish to be protected from some malevolent forces.

17. Do not be inflated and arrogant on account of your thought transformation practice.

18. Eliminate the ulterior motive which wishes others to suffer for the sake of your own happiness.

PRECEPTS OF THOUGHT TRANSFORMATION PRACTICE

1. Undertake all activities with the single thought to benefit others.

2. Oppose all interferences and enhance your practice through the altruistic attitude of equalizing and exchanging yourself with others.

3. Pursue all positive activities with the bodhicitta motivation at the beginning and a dedication at the end.

4. Transform all circumstances, both desirable and adverse, so that they become complementary to your practice of thought transformation.

5. Regard all pledges in general, and those of thought transformation in particular, as dear as your life.

6. Apply the appropriate opponent forces instantly when delusions arise and strive to sever their continuity.

7. Aggregate the three principle causes for your practice:
    a) proper reliance on an experienced spiritual guide;
    b) a mind receptive to righteous actions;

c) protection of the precepts of the three vows (individual liberation, bodhisattva, and tantra) from degeneration.

8. Maintain the three undeclining attitudes:

a) an undeclining devotion towards your spiritual mentor;

b) an undeclining joy in the practice of thought transformation;

c) an undeclining wish to observe the three vows.

9. Do not isolate your body, speech or mind from ethical conduct.

10. Always practice thought transformation with impartiality towards all.

11. Apply the thought transformation principles to all events.

12. Meditate with special attention on love and compassion towards your rivals, enemies, etc.

13. Always practice thought transformation without any dependence on favorableness in the external circumstances.

14. Exert yourself in the essence of the practice.

15. Abstain from six inverted deeds:

a) inverted patience: showing great patience for the hardships of mundane affairs rather than patience for the hardships of the cultivation of the altruistic aspiration.

b) inverted will: having great determination in pursuing meaningless worldly affairs, but having no such will towards the practice of dharma.

c) inverted taste: reveling in the enjoyment of pleasures derived through negative emotions such as desire, hatred, etc., rather than enjoying the bliss of meditation.

d) inverted compassion: feeling pity for a sincere dharma practitioner who is materially poor while admiring someone who is successful at the mundane level.

e) inverted loyalty: encouraging your close ones to pursue worldly involvements rather than guiding them to the path of dharma.

f) inverted rejoicing: rejoicing in the misfortunes of those whom you dislike, while remaining indifferent towards the positive actions of others which bring benefit to many.

16. Be steadfast and not intermittent in your practice.

17. Exert all your ability with single-pointedness and do not be plagued by doubts and hesitations.

18. Strive to eliminate your delusions through the constant application of examination and analysis.

19. Do not boast of the things done for others.

20. Do not be provoked by slight incidents and remarks.

21. Do not crave to receive gratitude and reputation because of your practice.

22. Do not be fickle.

Appendix II
Bodhisattva Vows

THE EIGHTEEN ROOT INFRACTIONS

1. Praising oneself and belittling others
2. Not sharing with others one's wealth and the dharma
3. Not forgiving even when others apologize
4. Doubting and denying the doctrine of the Great Vehicle
5. Taking offerings intended for the Three Jewels
6. Abandoning the doctrine (through sectarianism, etc.)
7. Causing an ordained person to disrobe
8. Committing one of the five crimes of immediate retribution
9. Holding perverted views
10. Destroying places such as towns
11. Teaching emptiness to those untrained
12. Discouraging others from seeking full enlightenment
13. Causing others to break the vows of individual liberation
14. Belittling those who follow the path of individual liberation
15. Proclaiming false realizations (of emptiness, etc.)
16. Accepting gifts of articles that have been misappropriated from the belongings of the Three Jewels

17. Laying down harmful regulations and passing false judgment

18. Giving up the pledge of altruistic aspiration (bodhicitta)

Except in the cases of giving up the pledge of altruistic aspiration and holding perverted views, a complete infraction of any of the root vows requires the association with what are called the "four factors for a thorough entanglement": (1) not being mindful of the disadvantages; (2) not reversing the desire to indulge in the infraction; (3) indulgence in the act with great pleasure and delight; and (4) lack of any shame and conscience.

THE FORTY-SIX SECONDARY INFRACTIONS

Seven downfalls related to generosity

1. Not making offerings every day to the Three Jewels

2. Acting out thoughts of desire because of discontent

3. Not paying due respect to those senior to one in ordination and in taking the bodhisattva vows

4. Not answering others' questions out of negligence though one is capable of doing so

5. Selfishly not accepting invitations due to pride, the wish hurt others' feelings, or anger and laziness

6. Not accepting others' gifts out of jealousy, anger, etc. or simply to hurt the other

7. Not giving the dharma teachings to those who wish to learn

Nine downfalls in relation to the practice of morality

1. Ignoring and insulting someone who has committed any of the five heinous crimes or defiled his/her vows of individual liberation, or treating him/her with contempt

2. Not observing the precepts of moral conduct because one wishes to ingratiate oneself with others

3. Complying with minor precepts when the situation demands one's disregard of them for the greater benefit of others

4. Not committing one of the seven negative actions of body and speech when universal love and compassion deem it necessary in a particular instance

5. Accepting things which are acquired through one of the five wrong livelihoods (flattery, hinting, bribery, extortion and deceit)

6. Wasting time on frivolous actions (such as carelessness, lack of pure morality, dancing, playing music just for fun, gossiping) and also distracting others in meditation

7. Misconceiving that bodhisattvas do not attempt to attain liberation and failing to view delusions as things to be eliminated

8. Not living up to one's precepts, thinking that doing so might decrease one's popularity, or not correcting the undisciplined behaviors of body and speech which result in a bad reputation that limits one's ability to carry out the tasks of a bodhisattva

9. Not correcting others who, motivated by delusions, commit negative actions. Doing so helps them to disclose and purify their actions, whereas concealing them generates suspicions of being disliked by others.

Four downfalls related to patience

1. Parting from the four noble disciplines: not retaliating when scolded by others, humiliated by others, hit by others or even when killed by others.

2. Neglecting those who are angry with you

3. Refusing to accept the apologies of others

4. Acting out thoughts of anger; not opposing the arousal of anger within one's mind by reflecting upon its harmful consequences, etc.

Three downfalls related to joyous effort

1. Gathering circles of disciples out of desire for respect and material gain

2. Wasting time and energy on trivial matters; not countering laziness, addiction to excessive sleep, and procrastination

3. Being addicted to frivolous talk

Three downfalls related to concentration
1. Not seeking the appropriate conditions for attaining a single-pointed concentration, and meditating on it without proper guidance
2. Not eliminating the obstacles to one's concentration
3. Regarding the blissful experience derived from concentration as the main purpose of single-pointed meditation

Eight downfalls related to wisdom
1. Abandoning the doctrines of the Lesser Vehicle with the thought that the practitioners of the Great Vehicle need not study or practice them
2. Unnecessarily expending one's energies in other directions despite having one's own Great Vehicle methods
3. Pursuing non-dharma studies to the neglect of the dharma ones
4. Studying non-dharma subjects with great thoroughness, out of attachment to these views, and favoring them
5. Abandoning the doctrines of the Great Vehicle, claiming that they are ineffective, and rejecting texts on grounds of their literary style
6. Praising oneself and belittling others out of arrogance or hatred
7. Not attending dharma ceremonies, discourses, etc. out of laziness or pride
8. Disparaging one's guru and not relying on his words

Twelve downfalls related to the ethics of helping others
1. Not helping those who need assistance
2. Avoiding the task of caring for sick people
3. Not working to alleviate others' suffering, such as the seven types of frustrations: being blind, deaf, lame, exhausted from fatigue, depressed, abused and rebuked by others, and suffering from the five hindrances to a calm and single-pointed mind

4. Not showing the dharma way to those recklessly caught up in the affairs of this life alone

5. Not repaying the kindness of others

6. Not consoling those who have mental grief, such as that caused by separation from loved ones

7. Not giving material aid to those who are in need of it

8. Not taking care of one's circle of disciples, relatives, and friends by giving them teaching and material aid

9. Not acting in accordance with others' wishes

10. Not praising those who deserve praise and their good qualities

11. Not preventing harmful acts to the extent permitted by circumstances

12. Not employing physical prowess or any supernatural powers, if one possesses them, at the time need.

Appendix III
Outline of Path to Bliss (Delam)

I. THE MODE OF RELYING ON A SPIRITUAL MASTER, THE FOUNDATION OF THE PATH

A. *Activities during the session*
  1. Preliminary activities
  2. Activities during main session
     a. Reliance through thought
     b. Reliance through action
        (1) Cultivating faith, the root factor
        (2) Cultivating respect through recollecting kindness
  3. Concluding activities
B. *Activities during between-session periods*

II. THE STAGES OF TRAINING THE MIND BASED ON SUCH A RELIANCE

A. *Persuading to take the essence of fully endowed human existence*
  1. Activities during the session
     a. Preliminaries
     b. The main session

(1) Reflecting on the great value of leisure and fortune

(2) Reflecting on its rarity

c. The concluding activities

B. *The manner in which to actually take the essence*

1. Training the mind in the stages of path common to the practitioners of initial capacity

a. Activities during the session

(1) Preliminaries

(2) The main session

(a) Meditation on death-awareness

(b) Reflecting on the sufferings of lower realms

(c) Taking refuge in the Three Jewels

(d) Generating conviction in the karmic law

(3) The concluding activities

b. Activities during between-session periods

2. Training the mind in the stages of path common to those of middle capacity

a. Generating the aspiration to achieve liberation

(1) Activities during the session

(a) Preliminaries

(b) The main session

i)Reflecting on the sufferings of cyclic existence in general

ii) Reflecting on the specific sufferings of individual realms

(c) The concluding activities

(2) Activities during between-session periods

b. Presentation of the nature of the paths leading to liberation

(1) Activities during the session

(a) Preliminaries

(b) The main session

(c) The concluding activities

(2) Activities during between-session periods

3. Training the mind in the stages of path common to
those of great capacity
  a. The mode of cultivating bodhicitta
    (1) The actual generation of the mind
      (a) Generating bodhicitta through the
instruction of seven-point cause and effect
        i) Meditation on equanimity
Preliminaries
The main session
The concluding activities
        ii) The seven-points
Recognition of all beings as having been
  one's mother
Recollection of their kindness
Repaying the kindness
Loving kindness
Great compassion
Superior attitude
Bodhicitta
      (b) Generating bodhicitta through the
instruction on equality and exchange of
oneself with others
        i) Activities during the session
Preliminaries
The main session
The concluding activities
        ii) Activities during between-session periods
    (2) Reinforcing the generated altruistic mind
through ceremony
      (c) Activities during the session
        i) Preliminaries
        ii) The main session
The way in which the vows are received
How to protect the vows from degeneration
        iii) The concluding activites
      (d) Activities during between-session periods

b. The mode of engaging in the deeds following the
generation of the altruistic mind
  (1) Training in the bodhisattva deeds in general
    (a) Activities during the session
      i) Preliminaries
      ii) The main session
        Generosity
        Morality
        Patience
        Joyous effort
        Concentration
        Wisdom
        The four ripening factors
      iii) The concluding activities
    (b) Activities during between-session periods
  (2) Training in the last two perfections in
  particular
    (a) Training in calm-abiding, the essence of
    concentration
      i) Activities during the session
        Preliminaries
        The main session
        The concluding activities
      ii) Activities during between-session periods
    (b) Training in special insight, the essence of
    wisdom
      i) Activities during the session
        Preliminaries
        The main session meditations
          On the selflessness of persons
          On the selflessness of phenomena
          On non-inherent existence of
            compounded phenomena
          On non-inherent existence of
            uncompounded phenomena
        The concluding activities
      ii) Activities during between-session periods

Notes

1. The full title of the text is *A Practical Guide on the Stages of the Path to Enlightenment: A Path of Bliss Leading to Omniscience (Jhangchup Lamgyi Rimpai Marti Thamche Khyenpar Droepai Delam She Jhawa)* by Panchen Lobsang Choekyi Gyaltsen.

2. The full title of this Lamrim text is *A Practical Guide to the Stages of the Path to Enlightenment: A Swift Path to Omniscience (Jhangchup Lamgyi Rimpai Marti Thamche Khyenpar Droepai Nyurlam She Jhawa)* by Panchen Palden Yeshi.

3. For the convenience of the readers, these repetitions have been incorporated into a single presentation in this book. The purpose of these repetitions during the oral teaching is to ensure that the listeners understand all the essential points of the particular section of meditation covered during the teaching session, so that the visualizations can be done without much difficulty. In order for disciples to receive an experiential commentary or guide on a given text, it is indispensible that they undertake the meditations explained in the teaching at least twice before the next day—once during the same evening and once the next morning.

4. A lucid commentary by H.H. the Dalai Lama on this important guru yoga text is available in English translation un-

der the title *The Union of Bliss and Emptiness* (Ithaca: Snow Lion Publications, 1988).

5. For the qualifications necessary on the part of the teacher in the context of specific practices, such as vinaya, Perfection Vehicle of Mahayana, and tantra, see *Union of Bliss and Emptiness*, p.123, and the translator's note on p.181.

6. The four trainings are discussed extensively in the fourth, fifth, sixth and seventh chapters respectively of the *Abhisamayalankara* (Ornament of Clear Realizations). For detailed explanations, see the root text and its related commentaries.

7. Buddhist literature speaks of all the different degrees of obstacles that impede one's spiritual transformation in terms of the "four maras" (negative influences). These are the negative influences of the aggregates; of delusions; of the divine youth; and of death. The first mara refers to the psychophysical aggregates which are the products of our delusions and negative karmic forces. The second refers to the negative emotions such as desire, hatred, jealousy, and anger that dominate our minds and bring harm. The third refers to spontaneous temptations that one normally feels regarding sensual pleasures; whereas the fourth mara refers to ordinary death, which is brought forth against our wishes as a consequence of our past actions, without any choice. For a detailed explanation on the definitions of the four maras and the spiritual levels at which they are overcome, see the fourth chapter of Maitreya's *Abhisamayalankara* (Ornament of Clear Realizations).

8. Clear Light is the subtlest level of mind, which becomes manifest only when all the gross minds have ceased their active functions. This state is experienced by ordinary beings naturally at the time of death, but can also be intentionally induced through meditative techniques. The reference here is to the latter.

9. The three kayas: dharmakaya (truth body), sambhogakaya (enjoyment body), and nirmanakaya (emanation body).

10. The outer refuge refers to the taking of refuge common to the practitioners of all the vehicles. It is the practice of simply going for refuge to the Three Jewels, induced by a sense of

fear for one's fate in the future and a deep conviction in the power of the Three Jewels to protect one from potential dangers. Inner refuge is an advanced form of the practice, uniquely used by the practitioners of the Great Vehicle. There are four features that distinguish it from the common refuge: (1) it should be induced by a sense of universal compassion, the taking into one's heart of the welfare of all beings; (2) the individual should be determined to attain full enlightenment; (3) the individual must have intellectually cognized the possibility of him or herself actualizing the state of the Three Jewels; and (4) it should transcend the refuge of the lesser vehicle practice. For explanations on these four features, see the second chapter of *Mahayana Sutralamkara* (Ornament of Great Vehicle Sutras) by Maitreya. The secret refuge refers to the practice of refuge in the context of the secret tantra path. It involves the taking of refuge not only in the Three Jewels but also in the assembly of mandala deities, which includes meditational deities, dakinis, heroes, etc.

11. Refutation that (1) the "self" is identical with the aggregates; (2) it is inherently different from the aggregates; (3) the aggregates are the base of the self; (4) the self is imposed on the aggregates; and (5) the self possesses the aggregates. For explanations on these five steps of reasoning, see *Meditation on Emptiness* by Jeffrey Hopkins (London: Wisdom Publications, 1983).

12. "Experiential Lineage" (*Nyamlen jhinlap gyue*) has different references, depending upon the context. Normally, it is identified with the lineage masters of the meditational deity in which the individual practitioner specializes. For a detailed explanation on the set-up of the merit field, see *Union of Bliss and Emptiness*, pp.62-91.

13. The five dhyani buddhas are Akshobya, Vairochana, Ratnasambhava, Amitabha, and Amogasiddhi, collectively known as the lords of the five buddha families. They are the purified states of the five aggregates: consciousness, form, feeling, discernment, and compositional factors.

14. The term *wisdom beings (yeshepas)*, refers to the deities

that are evoked from their natural abodes, such as the natural expanse of dharmakaya, and merge into the deity you have generated earlier. For instance, in the present context, the merit field that you have generated in a gradual sequence as described in the manual is the "commitment being." Once the visualization of the merit field is completed, you evoke "wisdom beings" identical to the set of merit field figures that you have already visualized, which are later merged into the commitment being. Such meditations are undertaken to reinforce your faith in and respect for the merit field created in your imagination.

15. See *Union of Bliss and Emptiness*, pp.62-91.

16. For a detailed explanation on the seven limbs, see *Union of Bliss and Emptiness*, pp.92-115.

17. The eight benefits are: (1) getting closer to the attainment of full enlightenment, (2) pleasing all the buddhas, (3) never being deprived of a spiritual mentor, (4) not falling into any realms of unfavorable transmigrations, (5) becoming impervious to misleading teachers and evil friends, (6) being able to withstand the afflictions of delusions and the negative karmic impulses, (7) enhancing the accumulation of merits as by always being mindful of the bodhisattva ideals and not acting against them, and (8) realizing all temporary and ultimate aims. For a detailed explanation, see Phabongkha's *Namdrol Lakchang*, published in English as *Liberation in Our Hands* (Howell, New Jersey: Mahayana Sutra and Tantra Press, 1990).

18. The eight undesirable consequences are: (1) despising one's spiritual guru yields results equal to those ensuing from showing contempt to all the buddhas; (2) by being angry towards one's guru, one destroys the positive potentials of the virtuous roots established over eons equal to the moments of the anger, and hence will take birth in the unfavorable realms of existence; (3) one will not attain any feats even by relying on tantric practices; (4) practicing tantra, even with great application, will be like working for one's own downfall; (5) no new knowledge will be developed and that already developed will degenerate; (6) in this life one will be tormented by un-

wanted experiences such as illness, etc.; (7) one will wander in the lower realms of existence for a long time; and (8) one will be deprived of a spiritual mentor in many future lives. For explanations, see Pabhongkha's *Namdrol Lakchang*.

19. Based on the difference in their presentation of the main subject matter, the entire corpus of the Buddha's teachings is categorized into three sets of discourses known as the Tripitaka, literally meaning the three baskets. These are the scriptural collections on (1) ethics, (2) discourses, and (3) knowledge, respectively dealing with the topics of the trainings in ethics, meditation and wisdom. For further explanation, see *Opening the Eye of New Awareness* by H.H. the Dalai Lama (London: Wisdom Publications, 1985), pp.48-51.

20. Some early Western writers on Tibetan Buddhism were mainly to blame for this mistaken image. Being aware only of the devotional aspects of Tibetan Buddhism and therefore the ritual aspect of tantra, these writers misunderstood Tibetan Buddhism as a degenerated form of Buddhism deeply imbedded in the native religion of Bon. Also, because in Buddhist tantra a special emphasis is placed on laying a proper foundation of a sound guru reliance practice, a spiritual mentor is regarded with the highest esteem, which may have contributed to the incorrect perception of Tibetan Buddhism as a degenerated Buddhism bordering on the practice of a personality cult. Such misunderstandings gave rise to the term *Lamaism*. Fortunately, as more and more literature on Tibetan Buddhism is becoming available now in English and other major languages, a genuine appreciation of the system is emerging.

21. The eight leisures or freedoms are the four freedoms from the bondage of non-human existence and the four from the obstacles found within human existence. They are (1) freedom from a birth as a hell being, (2) freedom from a birth as an animal, (3) freedom from a birth as a hungry spirit, (4) freedom from a birth as a long-life deva, (5) freedom from being born in a land where not even a word of the dharma is to be heard, (6) freedom from being born with impaired physical

and mental senses, (7) freedom from a rebirth holding perverted views such as disbelief in the karmic law of causality, and (8) freedom from being born at a time when a buddha has not appeared in the world.

22. The five personal endowments are (1) birth as a human being; (2) birth in a central land, a place where the dharma is present; (3) being born with complete sense faculties; (4) not having committed any of the five heinous crimes with immediate retribution (killing one's mother, father, a foe-destroyer, shedding the blood of a buddha with an intention to kill, and creating schism within a spiritual community); and (5) having faith in the three scriptural collections and dharma as a whole.

The five circumstantial endowments are: (1) birth at a time when a buddha has appeared on earth, (2) being born when the buddha has taught the dharma, (3) being born when this dharma is stable and flourishing, (4) being born when there are practitioners following the dharma, and (5) being born when there are kind benefactors who support the practitioners with material necessities.

23. The ten negative actions are as follows: three actions of body—killing, stealing and sexual misconduct; four of speech—lying, divisive talk, harsh speech and senseless gossip; and three of mind—covetousness, harmful intent and holding perverted views.

24. At the beginning of the spiritual path, based upon their diverse mental faculties, trainees are divided into three categories. Trainees whose spiritual endeavor is motivated principally to seek their own liberation from the bondage of cyclic existence are called *sravakas* (listeners); those who, although seeking their own welfare primarily, have a strong wish to be of service to others and have greater intelligence are called *pratyekabuddhas* (solitary realizers); and those who chiefly work for the attainment of the highest enlightenment to work for the benefit of others are the *bodhisattvas* (awakening warriors).

25. All the stages of one's journey towards enlightenment are included in five paths: (1) path of accumulation, (2) path

of preparation, (3) path of seeing, (4) path of meditation, (5) path of no more training. For an explanation on the five paths, see *Opening the Eye of New Awareness.*

26. The four powers are (1) the power of the basis, (2) the power of repentance, (3) the power of actual antidote, and (4) the power of resolve never to indulge in the acts again. For an explanation of these, see *Union of Bliss and Emptiness,* p.113.

27. Environmental effects are secondary effects of the karma that results externally on the natural environment in which one will incarnate in the coming life. Such an effect comes into fruition generally on a collective basis of many beings. For instance, our personal karma had some bearing upon the evolution of the planet earth.

28. The six types of suffering are those of (1) uncertainty, (2) lack of contentment, (3) having to discard the body again and again, (4) having to undergo conception repeatedly, (5) being subjected to repeated fluctuations, (6) lack of true companions.

The eight types of suffering are those of (1) birth, (2) aging, (3) illness, (4) death, (5) the frustrations of meeting the unwanted, (6) being separated from what is agreeable, (7) not obtaining what is desirable though one has sought it hard, and (8) in short, being bound to one's own five aggregates.

29. A commentary on this text in English is available under the title *Advice from a Spiritual Friend* by Geshe Rabten and Geshe Dhargyey (London: Wisdom Publications, 1986).

30. See Appendix I on thought transformation precepts.

31. *Union of Bliss and Emptiness,* pp.157-59

32. See *Bodhisattvacaryavatara,* chapter one, and its related commentaries.

33. The four negative actions are (1) deceiving one's gurus, or any beings worthy of veneration, by telling lies; (2) regretting one's positive actions and not one's negative actions; (3) despising bodhisattvas out of anger; and (4) being false and deceptive to any sentient being.

34. The four positive actions are (1) not telling lies even at the cost of one's life; (2) encouraging others in positive prin-

ciples, particularly the spiritual path of the Great Vehicle; (3) respecting all bodhisattvas as buddhas and proclaiming their great qualities; and (4) cherishing the special attitude of compassion towards all beings.

35. For the bodhisattva vows, see Appendix II.

36. For explanations on the different types of laziness and the factors that counter them, see *Meaningful to Behold* by Geshe Kelsang Gyatso (London: Tharpa Publications, 1989).

37. The eight opponent forces to the five obstacles:

THE EIGHT OPPONENT FORCES	THE FIVE OBSTACLES
1) Faith	1) Laziness
2) Aspiration	—
3) Joyous effort	—
4) Suppleness	—
5) Mindfulness	2) Forgetfulness
6) Introspection	3) Mental sinking and excitement
7) Application	4) Non-application of the antidotes
8) Non-application	5) Excessive application (equanimity)

For a detailed explanation of the eight opponent forces and the way in which they overcome the five obstacles, see Geshe Kelsang Gyatso's *Meaningful to Behold*, chapter eight.

38. The nine mental stages are (1) placing the mind, (2) continual placement, (3) replacement, (4) close placement, (5) controlled mind, (6) pacified mind, (7) complete pacification, (8) single-pointedness, and (9) equipoise.

For explanations on the nine stages, see Geshe Kelsang Gyatso's *Meaningful to Behold*, chapter eight.

Glossary

AGGREGATES   Form, feeling, discernment, compositional factors, and consciousness. These
faculties serve as the basis for the arisal
of an innate notion of self-identity in a
person. They are called aggregates because of their being composed through
the aggregation of many factors.

ARHAT   A spiritually matured being who has suc-
ceeded in rooting out from his or her
mental stream all delusions and the ignorance underlying them. Often this
Sanskrit term is translated into English
as *foe-destroyer; foe* here referring to delusions.

ASANA   Sanskrit word for the cross-legged posture of meditation: sometimes the term
is used in a metaphoric sense in a tantric context.

BHIKSHU   Sanskrit term for a fully ordained monk;
the female counterpart is Bhikshuni.

BODHICITTA   A spontaneous and non-simulated aspiration to attain full enlightenment for the

sake of all beings. This mental state can be generated through a process of intensive meditations based on a simulated universal love and compassion. The realization of bodhicitta marks the individual becoming a bodhisattva.

BODHISATTVA A spiritual trainee who has successfully generated a non-simulated aspiration to become fully enlightened for the benefit of all. *Bodhisattva* can be literally translated as "the awakening warrior."

BUDDHA A being who has become totally free of all limitations and is fully enlightened

CALM ABIDING A meditative state of mental absorption, accompanied by physical and mental suppleness, at which level one's mind has become extremely serviceable in focusing towards a chosen object. It is attained only through a successful development of the faculty of concentration, which one possesses within the mind. It is called *calm abiding* because it is a mental state where distractions by external objects are calmed and where the mind firmly abides on the chosen object of meditation.

CESSATION The third of the Four Noble Truths, a state of true cessation of sufferings and their causes

CLEAR LIGHT Clear Light is the subtlest level of mind, which becomes manifest only when all the gross minds have ceased their active functions. This state is experienced by ordinary beings naturally at the time of death, but can also be intentionally induced through meditative techniques.

CONSCIOUSNESS   In the Buddhist context, consciousness is used broadly to include all cognitive events and levels of the mind, even the very subtlest subconscious levels. Instinctive mental events and emotions also fall into this class of phenomena; thus animals are understood to possess consciousness.

DAKINI   Lit: Sky-goer. Class of female deities in Buddhist tantra embodying the wisdom aspect of the path.

DHARMA   This Sanskrit word has many different meanings. The most common usage denotes a "way of life" or "transformative process." In this context, it not only refers to the process itself but also to the transformed result as well. Hence *dharma* refers to the true paths and the true cessations to which the paths lead.

DHARMAKAYA   Truth body of the Buddha, the ultimate expanse into which all defilements are purified. It is also the basis or source from which the Buddha assumes varying physical manifestations suited to the differing mental dispositions of beings.

DHARMAPALAS   Wrathful deities who are assigned by highly realized beings to protect the doctrine

ENLIGHTENMENT   Used in Buddhist context to mean an awakened state of mind attained by an individual through a transformative process of spiritual purification. Thus *full enlightenment* refers to the total awakening of a Buddha.

FORM &
FORMLESS   The four form and four formless states are meditative states in which the attrac-

tion to external form is successively and eventually reduced to the point where the mind is totally withdrawn. Such meditative states lead to the practitioner's taking rebirths in form and formless realms.

FOUR NOBLE TRUTHS
The truths of (1) suffering, (2) its origin, (3) the cessation of suffering, and (4) the path which leads to the cessation of suffering.

FOUR CLASSES OF TANTRA
Action, performance, yoga, and highest yoga tantras

GREAT VEHICLE
Mahayana, the path of great capacity, that emphasizes others' welfare over one's own. It has two divisions: Perfection Vehicle and Tantric Vehicle.

GURU YOGA
Tantric meditation based on imagining one's own mind and body as inseparable from one's guru visualized as a meditational deity

ILLUSORY BODY
A very subtle body possessing specific characteristics assumed by a practitioner on a high level of completion stage in tantra. It is the main factor that purifies the ordinary intermediate state between death and rebirth.

KADAM
A tradition that originated from the teachings of Atisha in Tibet

KAYA
Sanskrit word for *body*, especially in the context of the different bodies of the Buddha, such as dharmakaya

LESSER VEHICLE
Hinayana, the path of beings with lesser capacity, and a system that concentrates more on individual liberation rather than a universal enlightenment for all

LIBERATION
In the Buddhist context, the term refers

	to a liberation from the bondage of delusion and sufferings in the cycle of existence.
LAMRIM	Stages of the path to enlightenment
MAHAYANA	*See* Great Vehicle
MADHAYAMIKA	A philosophical school of thought founded on
PRASANGIKA	the Emptiness doctrine of Nagarjuna by Buddhapalita and Chandrakirti in India
OMNISCIENCE	All-knowing wisdom of a buddha which is attained once all the obscurations to knowledge are removed from the mind
PERFECTION VEHICLE	Sutra system of the Great Vehicle, which emphasizes the practice of bodhisattva deeds within the scope of the six perfections
PROTECTOR	*See* Dharmapalas
PUJA	A ritual involving the making of ceremonial offerings to higher beings such as gurus, meditational deities, buddhas, etc.
PROSTRATION	A physical gesture of homage in which one touches one's palms, knees, and forehead to the ground in front of the object of homage
ROOT GURU	A person whom you have taken as your most important spiritual guide and mentor
SELFLESSNESS	Used as a synonym for *emptiness*. Refers to the identity-lessness of things, that is, to the fact that things have no inherently existing self nature.
THREE SCOPES	Initial, middling, and great capacities for the spiritual path

TWO TRUTHS · The dual aspect of all phenomena: the level of their appearance called conventional truth, and their ultimate reality known as ultimate truth

WISDOM BEINGS · Deities or buddhas evoked from their abodes in one's meditative visualization to merge with and inhabit their forms imagined earlier in the meditative sequence

Bibliography

Advice from a Spiritual Friend by Geshe Rabten and Geshe Ngawang Dhargye. London: Wisdom Publications, 1986.

Dode Drenpa Nyershag (The Sutra on Mindfulness).

Domsum Rabye (Divisions of the Three Vows), by Sakya Pandita.

Dulwai Do (The Condensed Essence of Discipline) Skt. *Vinayasutra*, by Gunaprabha.

Gaden Lhagyama (The Hundred Deities of the Joyous Land) by Dulnag Palden Sangpo.

Jhangchub Shunglam (The Main Path to Enlightenment) by Tsongkhapa.

Jhangchub Lamgyi Rimpai Marti Thamche Khyenpar Droepai Delam (A Practical Guide on the Stages of the Path to Enlightenment: A Path of Bliss Leading to Omniscience) by Panchen Lobsang Choekyi Gyaltsen.

Jhangchup Lamrim Chenmo (Great Exposition of the Stages of Path to Enlightenment) by Tsongkhapa.

Jhangchup Lamgyi Dronme (Lamp for the Path to Enlightenment) Skt. *Bodhipada-paradipa* by Atisha.

Jhangchup Sempai Choepa la Jugpa (A Guide to the Bodhisattva's Way of Life) Skt. *Bodhisattvacharyavatara* by Shantideva. English translation by Stephen Batchelor. Dharamsala: Library of Tibetan Works and Archives, 1979.

Jhangchup Sempai Sa (The Bodhisattva Grounds) Skt. *Bodhisattvabhumi* by Asanga.

Jhangchup Lamgyi Rimpai Marti Thamche Khyenpar Droepai Nyurlam (A Practical Guide on the Stages of the Path to Enlightenment: A Swift Path to Omniscience) by Panchen Losang Yeshe.

Jorchoe (The Six Preparatory Practices).

Lama Ngachupa (Fifty Verses on Guru Devotion) Skt. *Guru Panchashika* by Ashvagosha. English translation by Geshe Ngawang Dhargyey et al. Dharamsala: Library of Tibetan Works and Archives, 1975.

Lamgyi Tsowo Nampa Sum (Three Principal Aspects of the Path) by Tsongkhapa.

Lamrim Jampel Shalung (The Sacred Words of Manjushri) by H.H. the Fifth Dalai Lama.

Lamrim Namdrol Lagchang (Liberation in Our Hands) by Phabongkha Dechen Nyingpo. English translation by Geshe Lobsang Tharchin and Artemus B. Engle. Howell, New Jersey: Mahayana Sutra and Tantra Press, 1990.

Lamrim Nyamgur (Songs of Spiritual Experience) by Tsongkhapa.

Lamrim Sershunma (Essence of Refined Gold) by H.H. the Third Dalai Lama. See commentary of the same name by H.H. the Fourteenth Dalai Lama, edited by Glenn Mullin. Ithaca: Snow Lion Publications, 1985.

Lojong Dhondunma (Seven-Point Thought Transformation) by Chekhawa. See English translation and commentary in *Advice from a Spiritual Friend*, listed above.

Meaningful to Behold by Geshe Kelsang Gyatso. London: Tharpa Publications, 1989.

Meditation on Emptiness by Jeffrey Hopkins. London: Wisdom Publications, 1983.

Mitag Drenkul (Reminder of Impermanence) by Phabongkha Dechen Nyingpo.

Mitag Gomtsul Gyi Labjha (An Advice on How to Meditate on Impermanence) by Gungthang Tenpa Dronme.

Naljor Choepa Shigyapa (Four Hundred Verses on the Yogic Deeds) Skt. *Chatu-shataka Shastra* by Aryadeva.

Ngontogyen (Ornament of Clear Realizations) Skt. *Abhisamayalankara* by Maitreya.

Opening the Eye of New Awareness by H.H. the Dalai Lama. London: Wisdom Publications, 1985.

Sablam Lama Choepai Choga Detong Yerme (The Profound Path of Offering to the Gurus: Union of Bliss and Emptiness) by Panchen Lobsang Choekyi Gyaltsen. See commentary entitled *The Union of Bliss and Emptiness* listed below.

Sherchin Gyetongpa (The Perfection of Wisdom Sutra in Eight Thousand Lines). See translation by Edward Conze, *The Perfection of Wisdom Sutra in Eight Thousand Lines and Its Verse Summary*. Bolinas: Four Seasons Foundation, 1973.

Thekpa Chenpoi Gyue Lama (Unsurpassed Continnum of the Great Vehicle) Skt. *Uttaratantra* by Maitreya.

Tsema Namdrel (Thorough Exposition of Valid Cognitions) Skt. *Pramanavartika* by Dharmakirti.

Tsema Kunle Tuepa (Compendium on Valid Cognitions) Skt. *Pramana-samucca* by Dignaga.

Uma Rinchen Trengwa (Precious Garland) Skt. *Ratnavali* by Nagarjuna. English translation by Jeffrey Hopkins in *The Buddhism of Tibet* by the Fourteenth Dalai Lama. Ithaca: Snow Lion Publications, 1987.

Uma Gongpa Rabsel (Complete Elucidiation of the Intent) by Tsongkhapa.

Uma Tsawa Sherab (Fundamental Treatise on the Middle Way) Skt. *Mulamadhyamaka Karika* by Nagarjuna. In *Emptiness:*

A Study in Religious Meaning by Frederick Streng. Nashville: Abingdon Press, 1967.

Uma la Jugpa (Guide to the Middle Way) Skt. *Madhyamakavatara* by Chandrakirti.

The Union of Bliss and Emptiness by H.H. the Dalai Lama. Ithaca: Snow Lion Publications, 1988.

Yonten Shigyurma (Foundation of All Perfections) by Tsongkhapa.

Index